Judy 8 Nov. 1989

I thought [this?] be useful [when?] at the cottage.

Love
The Bretzloff's

BARBECUES
— AND —
OUTDOOR LIVING

AURA EDITIONS

Editor: Helen Davies
Art editor: Graham Beehag
Illustrations by Melanie Laslett

Published by Aura Editions,
2 Derby Road,
Greenford,
Middlesex

Produced by Marshall Cavendish Books Limited
58 Old Compton Street, London W1V 5PA

© Marshall Cavendish Limited 1986

ISBN 0 86307 438 3

Phototypeset in Souvenir by
Quadraset Limited, Avon

Printed and bound in Italy by
L.E.G.O. s.p.a.

INTRODUCTION

Cooking in the open air is one of the delights of summer — food always seems to be full of flavour when eaten out of doors. *Barbecues and Outdoor Living* gives you all the information you need to make your barbecue parties a success, from preparing tasty dishes to making attractive and practical outdoor furniture.

The first choice you'll have to make is what kind of barbecue to buy or build — portable or permanent, charcoal or gas. A comprehensive guide to all the most popular types is included, together with information on equipment and accessories. Cooking on an open fire is a skill anyone can learn, provided a few simple guidelines are followed. We show you how to get the best out of your barbecue and remind you of some important safety watchpoints.

Garden furniture is an important part of outdoor entertaining. As it can be expensive to buy, why not make your own? You can start with a simple patio table, or build a picnic table and benches. We also show you how to plan a patio and give tips on garden lighting.

The recipe section contains a range of tasty and appetising dishes which can be put together with the minimum of fuss. Salads and starters accompany the varied meat and fish dishes, many of which can be made in advance. Delicious desserts are also featured, to complete the menu.

All the recipes and projects are illustrated in full colour and include clear instructions and Cook's Notes.

CONTENTS

BARBECUES AND EQUIPMENT

Buying the right barbecue can be difficult — there are so many different types to choose from. To help you make up your mind we show you the most popular models and explain how to use them. Accessories and equipment are covered in detail, together with step-by-step instructions on building your own barbecue unit.

CHOOSING A BARBECUE

A barbecue is a welcome addition to any garden, large or small — from a postage stamp-sized city back yard to a more spacious garden with lawns and a patio. Because tasty food can be cooked on the smallest of portable grills, anyone who has access to a patch of ground outdoors — so long as it's not closely overhung with trees — can try their hand at barbecuing. Even flat-dwellers without gardens or patios needn't despair because simple picnic barbecues are available, which are ideal for outdoor holidays, or for a day on the beach or in the country.

Before you buy your first barbecue, it is a good idea to think carefully about how often you will use it, its site — whether in the garden or on a patio — and how many people you will usually be cooking for. At first you may decide to buy a simple picnic or brazier model (see below) and then graduate to a more sophisticated design in a later season. Whichever type you choose, make sure it feels solid and stable — so that not only will you feel confident when using it, but your guests too can happily be left to take a turn at the grill — leaving you free to greet friends, dispense drinks or just relax!

Outlined below are the main types of barbecue, most of which are fuelled by solid fuel: either charcoal briquettes or charcoal lumps.

Picnics and braziers

The circular, tripod-like barbecues, which are called 'picnic' barbecues, and their more sophisticated cousins — the braziers (or 'party' barbecues) — are among the basic models. Not only are they ideal for beginners, but — because they are so versatile — they will certainly see you through a couple of summers — and lots of entertaining!

Picnic barbecues: these consist of a circular drip pan with a maximum

The grill pan of this brazier barbecue has handles, which makes for safe lifting. It is also on wheels — useful for moving it around in the garden

diameter of 460 mm (18 in). An adjustable grill fits into notches on a windshield, which can hold skewers for kebabs. Some models have folding legs so they can be carried in a car or even strapped to a back-pack. The grill pan on a picnic barbecue should provide enough room for food for six to eight people.
Braziers: these may also be called 'party' barbecues — perhaps because

the larger grill makes it possible for guests to cluster round and take turns with the cooking! They can be either circular or rectangular, the circular grills vary in diameter from 460 mm to 610 mm (18 to 24 in) and most types have folding or screw-in legs. Spits for kebabs slot into a windshield, and some models come complete with a rotisserie. There is usually an adjustable shelf between the legs which is useful for storing plates and food.

Hibachis

'Hibachi' is the Japanese word for 'fire bowl'; anyone who is cramped for space will find a hibachi particularly suitable. It consists of a firebox with small, squat legs and is placed on a wall or other fire-proof surface for cooking. The most durable hibachis are made from cast-iron, although sturdy models made from

The compact hibachi barbecue has short, square legs and is usually placed on a wall or table for cooking. Double and triple versions are available

pressed-steel and aluminium are also available. The fire bowl — which comes with a grill — should be at least 80 mm (3 in) deep; double and triple versions are also available. The fire bowl is round or rectangular, and has draught controls to help with lighting and fanning the coals. Like the simpler of the brazier models, the hibachi is excellent for beginners.

Hooded barbecues

These are larger versions of the circular or rectangular brazier barbecue, with the added refinement of a hood which not only keeps smoke out of the guests' faces but also protects the food when cooking. The hood can also be closed down for smoke cooking (see also Kettle barbecues). When open the barbecue may take a spit attachment, normally operated by a battery-driven motor. Most hooded barbecues have shelves and the legs may be on wheels.

With two spit attachments and notches for skewers, this wagon barbecue is ideal for spit roasting and kebabs. Like most wagons it is on wheels and has a storage shelf

Wagon barbecues

Wagons are usually rectangular and are mounted on a trolley for mobility. Most models have some storage space — either at the sides or beneath — and notches for holding spits or a rotisserie. The grill area on a wagon barbecue is usually large so it is possible to cater for a big party. Because of its construction this type of barbecue is fairly heavy, so it is sensible to place carefully: either on a paved area or patio.

Kettle barbecues

The ultimate in barbecue sophistication, kettles are spherical and are made of heavy-gauge steel finished in porcelain enamel — often in bright colours. They range in size from a small portable model at 370 mm (14½ in) which can cope with small roasts, to 940 mm (37 in) which can

This hooded barbecue can be used either as an oven or a grill. Its air vent (inset) opens or closes to control the heat during cooking

cook several joints of meat at a time. When the lid is closed, the kettle acts like an oven and the warm air circulates inside to roast the food; when the lid is open, it can be used like a brazier with a spit or a rotisserie.

The kettle is not only versatile, it is also economical: when the air vents in the lid are closed, the fire dies down and the fuel can be used again. It is excellent for the smoke cooking of meat and fish: the smoky taste can be achieved by adding dampened hickory chips to the hot coals and closing the lid.

'No fuss' barbecuing

For those who enjoy the flavour of barbecue-cooked food, but would rather avoid the delay of waiting for the fuel to heat up, then the alternative is to buy a model powered by gas or electricity. Both wagon and kettle barbecues are available in gas-powered versions, as is a table-top portable gas grill, which has folding legs for storage. In this particular model the heat comes from a gas burner fed by butane gas (available in a canister). This heats a rack filled with volcanic rocks and so provides heat for cooking.

Electric barbecues — usually in the form of a table-top grill — are also available; heated by an electric element they will be hot enough to cook on ten minutes after being switched on. Unlike gas models they do not create poisonous fumes and so can be used indoors; like the gas versions, they have the advantage of producing mouth-watering food.

WATCHPOINT

Charcoal and gas barbecues are not safe to use either indoors or in a covered conservatory. If it starts to rain, the only safe spot undercover is the very edge of a brick-built garage.

You can cook up a feast on a kettle barbecue with the minimum of fuss — this attractive model can cope with a rib of beef, burgers, sausages and stuffed peppers — with room to spare!

Permanent barbecues

If you're going to use your barbecue regularly, and you've got sufficient space, you might consider erecting a brick-built barbecue. A solid surface — made from concrete or paving slabs — is essential. Instructions for building an attractive barbecue — with its own serving area — are given on pages 16–21.

An alternative to building your own from scratch is to use one of the do-it-yourself kits that are on the market. These supply the grill-pan, fire box and ash pan — all you have to do is supply the bricks. For more information, and step-by-step instructions, see page 15.

This gas barbecue works by heating up the natural lava rock in its base. Both gas and electric barbecues are warmed much more quickly than those powered by charcoal; but those without lava rock do not give a charcoal flavour to the food

USING THE BARBECUE

A barbecue party should be an informal occasion when friends and family can get together and relax in the open air. But like all the best parties, a little forward planning and attention to detail is essential.

The perfect site

Position your barbecue carefully — the illustration below shows the perfect site. A solid, level surface is essential — either a paved area like a patio or a patch of concrete or gravel. The barbecue should be kept well away from overhanging trees, bushes or beds with tall flowers. If possible, place it against a wall (not a wooden fence) to keep it out of the prevailing wind.

The barbecue should not be sited on a path or an area where guests are likely to be walking backwards and forwards. It's a good idea to have a table next to the barbecue for basic utensils and serving — but keep drinks, salads and other food separate from the cooking area to give the chef plenty of space to work.

It is not a good idea to use the barbecue table for serving drinks. This encourages guests to mill around where the chef is working; instead, place the serving table inside the house.

The different fuels

There are three types of fuel which are commonly used in barbecue cooking: charcoal lumps, charcoal briquettes and hickory wood.

Charcoal lumps: this is the cheapest and most popular form of barbecue fuel. It lights easily and burns quickly, so is good for fast cooking. However, if you plan to cook over a couple of hours — during the length of an evening, for example — you will need to refuel the fire. When you are buying lump charcoal make sure that it is light and dry, with the minimum of dust in the bottom of the bag.

Charcoal briquettes: these are more expensive than lumps but burn roughly twice as long. They are worth the extra expense because the chef will not have to stop cooking to re-fuel the fire. Briquettes are an even shape and produce a good heat without causing sparks.

Hickory wood: this particular hardwood can be used to fuel the barbecue and gives the food a delicious smoky flavour. But it is an expensive form of fuel, so hickory chips are usually just scattered on the coals before cooking starts. If you plan to use these chips they should be soaked in water for half an hour before use.

An open paved area, well away from overhanging trees, shrubs and tall flowers, is the ideal spot for the barbecue

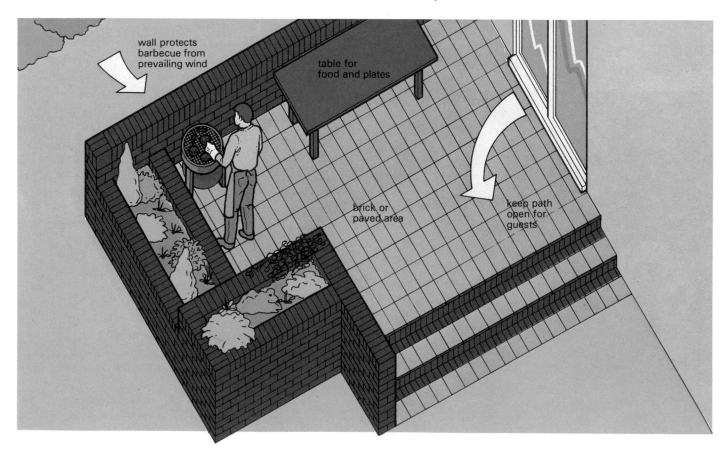

wall protects barbecue from prevailing wind

table for food and plates

brick or paved area

keep path open for guests

Lighting the barbecue

Unless you have a gas or electric model, it's essential to light the barbecue at least 45 minutes before you start cooking — it will take this time for the coals to reach the required temperature. Before filling the firebox with charcoal, line it with thick aluminium foil, shiny side up. This will protect the barbecue, and make it easier to remove the ash. Next, spread a layer of fine gravel or vermiculite (sometimes called 'barbecue base' when it is sold) on top of the foil. This supports the charcoal and allows air to pass through so that the fire burns more evenly.

You will also need to use one of the proprietary firelighters that are sold to get the fire started — in fact, it's almost impossible to ignite the coals without them. There are two types: solid firelighters, and liquid fuel which is sold in bottles and sachets. Never use petrol, lighter fuel, naphtha or paraffin (kerosene) as they are too volatile and may also taint the flavour of the food.

Whichever type of firelighter you choose, the technique of lighting the fire is the same. A pyramid of charcoal should be built in the centre of the firebox. If you are using solid firelighters, break one of these up into two or three pieces and place them just above the bottom layer of charcoal. Liquid sachets should be tucked between the coals in roughly the same position while bottled liquid starter should be sprayed over the top of the coals once the pyramid is in position.

Light the fire with a taper — never use a match. Once the firelighters

Left to right: briquettes, hickory chips and charcoal lumps

Tuck pieces of firelighter in the base of the pyramid . . .

. . . or place sachets of liquid firelighter in the same place

. . . or spray bottled starter on top of the coals

11

that they will be too hot for cooking and you will burn the food.

SAFETY WATCHPOINTS

● Set your barbecue up on a solid surface, well away from overhanging trees, bushes or flowerbeds (see illustration on previous page). Position it behind a low wall out of the prevailing wind. Never place it on a path where guests will be walking to and fro.

● Use only the recommended quantity of starter fuel or firelighters. Apart from the danger of flare-ups, this fuel can often taint the food.

● Never pour petrol or paraffin (kerosene) over the coals to help them ignite. The heat should be allowed to spread naturally from one coal to the next.

● Have a garden handspray close by to control flare-ups.

● Have a large metal dustbin lid (or similar) close by to smother a fire that gets out of control.

● Always wear gloves and an apron when tending the barbecue.

BARBECUE DO'S AND DON'TS

● Do keep a close eye on children.
● Do keep pets indoors.
● Don't scorch your grass or paving stones.
● Don't splash fat onto the patio or paving stones.
● Don't throw rubbish onto the fire of the barbecue.
● Don't leave the barbecue unsupervised.

Controlling the heat

Unless you control the fire carefully, it is very easy for it to get out of hand. On most barbecues you can alter the distance between the grill and the fire to raise or lower the heat. On kettle barbecues you can also control the heat by opening and closing the air

Control flare-ups using a hand-held spray. Take care not to splash dust on the food

ignite you should see smoke begin to rise from the centre of the pile. This will disappear after about 15 minutes by which time the coals will have gradually begun to transfer their heat from one to the other, starting from the centre. Slowly add more charcoal around the outside.

At first the coals will glow red; after about half an hour they will turn grey. This is the sign that you are ready to start cooking. You can also test to see if the fire is hot enough by

Test the heat by holding your hand — cautiously — over the grill. If you can stand it for two or three seconds, the fire is hot; four seconds and it's warm; five seconds and it's low

holding your hand about four inches above the coals. If you can't keep your hand there for more than two or three seconds, then the coals have reached the required temperature. Do not allow the coals to warm up beyond this stage, as you will find

vents: the more air you allow in, the stronger the fire will be. Flare-ups, which occur when hot fat drips onto the coals, should be controlled with a small garden hand spray. But take care when you use the spray not to kick dust onto the food.

When adding charcoal to the fire, place it at the sides rather than in the centre and it will gradually warm up. Remember that the closer together you place the coals, the more intense will be the resulting heat.

A double layer of aluminium foil, placed shiny side up in the fire box, will protect the base and help spread the heat

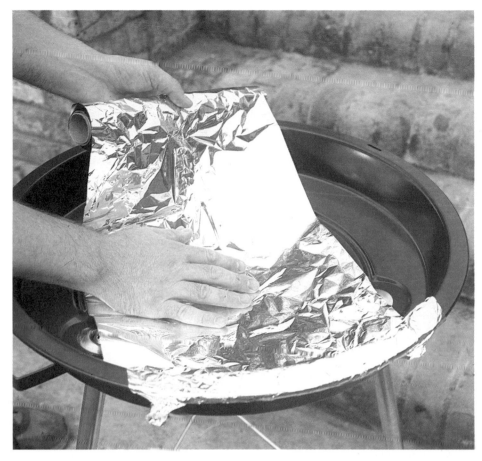

WATCHPOINT

Always wear gloves and an apron when cooking. Even though the day may be warm, try to wear long sleeves. If guests feel like trying their hand at the grill, insist that they too don the apron and gloves — this will keep them safe, and they will thank you for protecting their party clothes!

Barbecue maintenance

After you have finished cooking, allow the fire to die down completely; never try to douse it with a bucket of water. When the coals are completely cool, empty out the ash and base material and remove the foil. Clean the firebox with an oven or barbecue cleaner and a stiff brush. At the end of the season, store all your equipment under cover — this will prolong its life.

Barbecue accessories

The items that every barbecue cook should have are listed below. All the equipment that is used for turning the food on the grill and for basting should be long-handled, to prevent accidental burns.

● Long-handled tongs — two pairs, one for the coals, one for the food.
● Long-handled fork — to move the food on the grid.

After use, clean the firebox, drip pan, grill, spit and skewers with an oven cleaner and a stiff brush. Store under cover at the end of the season

- Long-handled brush — for swishing on sauces and marinades.
- Long-handled fish slice — for turning.
- Plenty of aluminium foil, for lining the barbecue base and for wrapping food for cooking.
- Skewers for kebabs — these should be flat so the kebabs can be turned easily.
- Wire baskets for cooking fish and steaks.
- A spit basket which attaches to the spit rod for cooking poultry.
- Meat thermometer — to ensure that the inside of the meat and poultry is properly cooked (especially important in outdoor cookery where meat may look done on the outside but may be under-cooked inside).
- Sharp knives for carving and chopping, plus a chopping board.

Other equipment

- Large waste bin — for paper napkins, paper plates, cups etc.
- Bug repellant spray — to deter the insects which will be attracted by the food and lights — but avoid squirting over the food! (Note too that aerosol sprays should be kept clear of the fire.)
- First aid kit — including burn lotion, plasters and antiseptic.

Above right: insect repellant in the form of a candle, to keep bugs at bay. Right: this rotisserie is powered by a battery-driven motor. Below left: a vermiculite base increases the supply of air to the coals. Below right: long-handled accessories are essential for safe barbecuing. Use a hand-held garden spray to control flare-ups

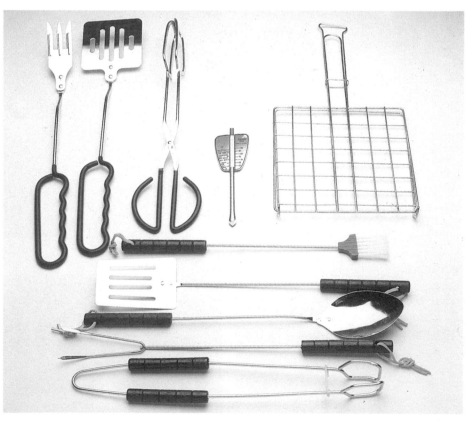

BARBECUE KITS

For those who would like to have a permanent barbecue, yet who do not wish to design the structure, a barbecue kit may be the answer. A number of different-sized kits are available, some of which have rotisseries and spits, and some with gas burners. The kits come with grill pan, fire box and an ashpan, but you have to provide the bricks.

The metal parts are supported by brackets which should be inserted into the joints of the bricks. Make sure these are correctly spaced and securely positioned for safety.

You can assemble the barbecue 'dry' by just building up the bricks, so that you can remove it later on. But if you decide to mortar the bricks in, you will need to make a 4:1 sand/cement mix. Select the spot carefully — perhaps experimenting with a portable barbecue first. If possible, choose a paved area or a patch of concrete, preferably building against a brick wall or corner for safety.

You may decide that you would like to design a patio which will incorporate the barbecue; for more information see pages 27–31.

1 Use the grill pan as a guide to the size of the barbecue when laying the first course of bricks

2 Build upwards, spanning one brick half across another. You will have to cut some bricks in half

3 Working on a flat surface, cut the bricks with a hammer and bolster. Use another brick as a cutting guide

4 Hold the bolster on the middle of the brick and give it a clean blow. You may have to tidy the edges of the cut brick afterwards

5 All the metal parts of the barbecue are supported on small metal brackets which are inserted between the bricks at the appropriate intervals

6 Place the grill, firebox and ash pan at the appropriate levels. Check that the whole structure is secure before you begin cooking

BUILD A BARBECUE UNIT

The 'build-it-yourself' barbecue unit itself is basically an H-shaped brick base with a slatted table on top, set at a convenient and comfortable height for food preparation and eating. It can be used with either a charcoal-fuelled grill or a gas cylinder, which you remove when the party's over.

The main design feature is a spacious surround which can be a serving area, dining table or bar. There's ample room to prepare the food, space underneath for storing implements, charcoal or gas cylinders — and there's even provision for a hot plate.

Ready-made barbecue grills, on which you actually cook the food, are designed to operate efficiently, so why try to better their performance with a home-made one? Either you end up with a makeshift arrangement or you have to get involved in complicated metalworking. This design avoids all that. You simply sit your choice of portable barbecue complete on the shelf near the top of the unit and either connect it up to the gas cylinder underneath or make up a fire with either charcoal lumps or briquettes.

Planning points

The brick-built barbecue will be quite a prominent feature in the garden so choose the site carefully. It should be on fairly level ground and reasonably sheltered — but, for safety, not directly underneath overhanging branches or too close to the house. There should be enough space behind for you to cook and plenty of room around the other sides for your guests to sit on bar stools.

If you want to build on an existing base, there may be sufficient room on your patio or other paved area. A single slab will almost certainly be solid enough, but if you are building on pavers check that they are firm and sound. If no existing surface is

suitable for building the unit on you'll have to allow for making new concrete foundations. These can be just large enough to take the barbecue itself, or bigger, to provide a solid platform around it. You can lay paving around it or make it the centrepiece of a new patio.

The sizes for the unit given here are not hard and fast: you can make a smaller or a larger one, depending on the space you have available and the extent of your entertaining. If you do need to alter the sizes, however, try to do so in steps of 75 mm — the thickness of a brick plus one mortar course.

When you buy your bricks try to choose ones that match or blend with adjacent brickwork — on a garden wall, your house, or paved areas, for instance — as this helps to give the impression of purposeful, sympathetic design. Keep a look out for a

demolition site if you want 'old', weathered bricks, which you can often obtain in reasonable condition (although you'll have to arrange your own collection); or simply order a new load from a local brick merchant.

The barbecue featured here is designed to keep the brickwork simple. If you modify it, you may have to change the arrangement. You can lay the bricks in a variety of bonding patterns but try to avoid too many cut bricks — these only weaken the strength of the structure and tend to look messy. Dry-lay the first few courses of bricks to check that your arrangement works.

Treat the timberwork — like the masonry — to match or contrast with surrounding features. You can paint it, stain it, or even simply sand it and treat it with linseed or vegetable oil. But don't use preservative on the slats because it could possibly contaminate the food.

What to buy

If you're making new foundations for the barbecue you'll need a fairly coarse concrete mix — buy the dry ingredients ready-mixed in bags, and simply add water. Two 50 kg (110 lb) bags of concrete will be adequate unless you want a large paved area. You also need dry-mixed bricklaying mortar for laying the bricks — two 50 kg (110 lb) bags should be ample.

As for the number of bricks, allow 265 for the standard unit, including extra for the inevitable breakages which occur when cutting.

Choose planed-all-round (PAR) softwood for the frame of the bench top. Don't use the cheaper sawn timber; people sitting at the bar are likely to get splinters in their knees from its underside. All timber except for the slats should be preservative-treated — it's best to soak the ends in the liquid for maximum penetration.

To make the table top, barbecue shelf and equipment shelf for the standard unit, you'll need to buy the following materials:
● 4.5 m of 75 mm × 25 mm timber to make the formwork.
● 4 m of 75 mm × 50 mm timber for the main frame.
● 2.6 m of 75 mm × 15 mm timber for the barbecue shelf, with two end pieces of 50 mm × 50 mm, each 375 mm long; 1.6 m of 75 mm × 50 mm for the support battens.

This stylish barbecue, with its top finished in slatted wood, could even double as an outdoor dining table

● Eight 50 mm × 250 mm of 19 mm exterior grade chipboard for the utensil shelf.

To assemble the timber frame you need glue and 38 mm long No. 8 countersunk woodscrews — make sure you buy an exterior woodworking adhesive. The frame itself is secured to the brickwork with twelve 100 mm long screws driven into masonry plugs. Attach the slats to the frame with 25 mm oval nails. It is not necessary, but it is a good idea, to use sherardized screws and nails to avoid rusting.

Building the brick base

If you aren't building onto an existing patio or slab the first thing to do is to make firm foundations for your unit; then you can lay the brick course for the barbecue base.

The foundations consist of a specially prepared surface of well-rammed hardcore topped with concrete. Start the job by marking out with string where your barbecue base will go. The drawing on pages 18–19 shows the area it covers. Add about 300 mm all round for working space and dig out the topsoil and any roots or grass within this rectangle to a depth of 150 mm — or 200 mm if soil is very light and sandy. Level off the excavation roughly and cut the edges with your spade to make sure that they're clean and straight.

Spread gravel, stones and old broken bricks (hardcore) to a thickness of about 75 mm in the shallow pit you've dug. Tamp it down to compact it with a stout piece of timber, used end on — a fence post is ideal for this job.

Concrete tends to 'slump' while it's setting so you'll need a mould or 'formwork' to retain and support the mix. Make this from four lengths of 75 mm × 25 mm timber nailed together to form a frame that has internal dimensions of 1390 mm ×

715 mm. Check that it's square with a try square and temporarily nail diagonal braces across the corners to make sure it stays that way.

Lay the frame on top of the gravel precisely where your barbecue is to stand. Lay a spirit level along the top and wedge the frame with bricks or pieces of wood until it is level in all directions. If the ground slopes at all make sure that the top of the box is level with the lowest part of the slope — so as to hide the unfinished slab. It's a good idea to drive wooden pegs into the ground at the perimeter of the formwork to hold the box more firmly in position.

WATCHPOINT

If you've used large-sized gravel and brick that's difficult to compact, sprinkle a few shovelfuls of sand into the box and spread it out to fill up the bigger voids, which would be wasteful of concrete. It helps if you break up the larger pieces as much as you can in the first place.

Don't try to lay your concrete if there is a risk of frost. There's a danger that if it freezes, the slab may crack. If the weather is very hot, on the other hand, you must cover the slab to prevent it from drying out too quickly and cracking.

Lay a piece of board down to give you a conveniently close working surface. Mix up the concrete following the instructions on the bag and keeping it as dry as possible. Shovel it into the box, working it into the edges and tamp it well down using a stout straight-edged board. Check the formwork to make sure it's still level and square, then scrape off the concrete level with the top by drawing the board across. The surface can be fairly rough-and-ready as its purpose is only to provide a firm surface for the bricks. Nevertheless, it should be square and level. Minutes spent on getting it right now will save hours later trying

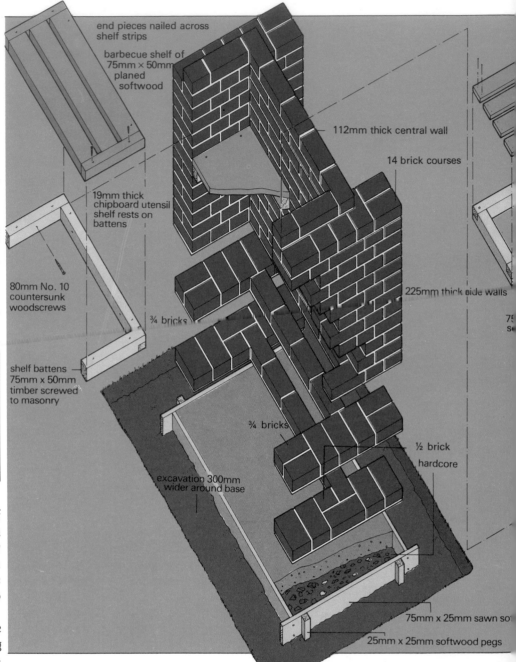

Labels in illustration: end pieces nailed across shelf strips; barbecue shelf of 75mm × 50mm planed softwood; 19mm thick chipboard utensil shelf rests on battens; 80mm No. 10 countersunk woodscrews; shelf battens 75mm x 50mm timber screwed to masonry; ¾ bricks; excavation 300mm wider around base; 112mm thick central wall; 14 brick courses; 225mm thick side walls; ¾ bricks; ½ brick; hardcore; 75mm x 25mm sawn softwood; 25mm x 25mm softwood pegs

to correct unevenness in the brickwork. And if you want to give any special finish to the slab, such as tiling over it, you will need a firm, flat surface as a base.

Cover your concrete slab with plastic sheeting or a wet hessian bag and leave it to set. After a few days you can remove the covering and start bricklaying. There's no need to

A concrete foundation slab, where necessary, can be built over a bed of hardcore

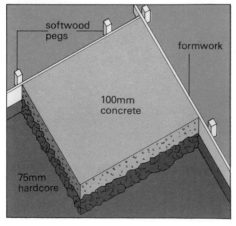

Labels in illustration: softwood pegs; formwork; 100mm concrete; 75mm hardcore

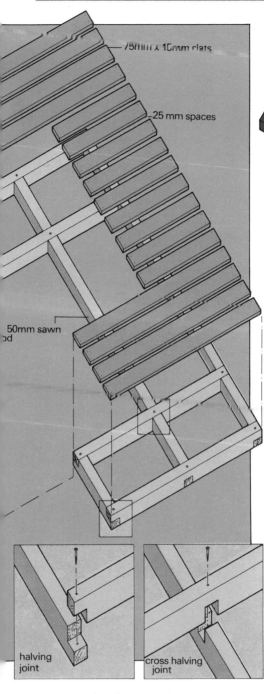

75mm x 10mm slats

25 mm spaces

50mm sawn
od

halving
joint

cross halving
joint

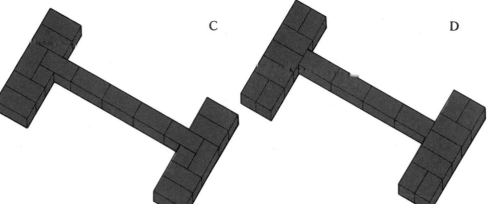

C

D

The pattern of the first course of bricks and each alternate course. Two half bricks are required

The pattern used for the second course of bricks and the alternate courses can be laid without cutting any bricks

1 Trowel a bed of mortar onto the slab and lay the bricks with 100 mm gaps between

2 Lay the second course of bricks (using the pattern above), checking level and alignment

remove the formwork box yet; you can use it as a base line for measuring the height of the brick courses.

Stack your bricks near to hand, ready for laying. Sort out any that are damaged — chipped corners can be disguised by putting them to the centre of the end walls. Dampen the bricks before laying — it makes them easier to lay and stops them drying the mortar too quickly.

Lay the bricks of the first course — see the diagram above — with a 10 mm space between each one.

3 Build up the 255 mm thick brick walls at the ends first, checking they are level

4 Insert the bricks at the ends of the 112 mm thick connecting wall. Tie each alternate row into the wall

5 Continue building across the centre of the connecting wall

6 As you build up, check from time to time that the walls are square and plumb with a spirit level

7 The final course is set back to provide a ledge against which to fix the shelf top

The most accurate laying routine is to lay the 225 mm thick single brick walls first, check that they're level and square, then lay the 112 mm thick, half-brick wall connecting them. If you are in doubt at any point, dry-lay the bricks first to check their exact position.

The bonding pattern is designed for simplicity as well as strength — and to economize on cut bricks. But you still need to cut a fair number. Where this is necessary use a bricklaying bolster and club hammer. Put the cut end inwards to disguise it.

To ensure that the bricks are bedded accurately on the foundation, trowel mortar along one edge and furrow the surface by drawing your trowel back along the screed in ripples; not only does this help you to position the bricks accurately but it also aids adhesion of the mortar through suction.

Check that the bricks line up on the outside edge and that they form a level course by holding your spirit level at the sides and on top. Tap any badly misaligned bricks into place with the handle of the trowel. If any are too low, add more mortar underneath to make up the gap.

Lay the second course (D in the diagram) by scooping trowel loads of mortar on top of the first row of bricks. Continue in this way, alternating courses C and D, checking that the joint thickness is constant. From time to time check the brickwork isn't bowing outwards by holding the level diagonally across the wall. Build the wall up until you reach course fourteen. Above this, a final half-brick course is set on top, within the slatted gap.

Assemble the shelf from three lengths of 100 mm × 50 mm softwood glued together and held by two 50 mm × 50 mm pieces nailed across their ends. The shelf simply rests on 75 mm × 50 mm timber battens at course eleven, but don't try to fix them in place until the mortar has hardened.

A chipboard utensil shelf rests on battens at course nine, but because it does not have to support heavy objects you could simply use metal angle brackets.

Tidy up the mortar courses when the mortar has begun to dry by rubbing them with a length of dowel or plastic hose to form round-profile joints. You needn't 'point' the joints on the inside or back of the unit; simply brush them down to remove excess mortar. Clean down the rest of the brickwork when the mortar has stiffened with a stiff-bristled hand brush, chipping off any excess mortar that has gone hard using a bolster chisel or wire brush.

Remove the formwork box by knocking apart the sides and clean up any mortar droppings from the ground surrounding the unit. Then shovel back the margin of earth you dug out beyond the foundation. Be careful with the concrete edges — they'll still be quite weak. If there's any likelihood of frost over the next few days it is advisable to cover your brickwork with a polyethylene sheet to prevent the mortar from cracking.

Leave the brick unit for approximately two days so that the mortar will harden fully, then screw on the slatted timber top.

Making halving joints

Halving joints are formed by two rebates, each half the thickness of the wood. When fixed together the original thickness of the timber is restored. The joint is strong, and ideal for making frameworks, especially where the joints are to be on show as in this project.

To make a corner halving joint first mark in pencil the width of each piece of wood on the other. Continue the lines around the two adjacent sides of both pieces of wood. This gives you the correct width of the joint.

It's best for accuracy to mark out and cut the width lines of both parts of the corner halving joints with the components clamped together on a workbench.

Mark the thickness of the joint by setting a marking gauge to half the thickness of the wood and scribe the line over the end of the wood and down to each width line.

Clamp the wood upright and cut down the thickness line to the width line. Remember to saw on the waste side of the line in case the saw should 'stray' and remove too much. It's best to start with the saw at an angle, gradually becoming horizontal.

Place the wood on a flat surface and saw down the width line to remove the waste wood. Repeat this procedure for the other half of the joint. Sand each meeting face of the joint and apply woodworking adhesive. You can simply nail the joint to hold it, but a stronger joint uses screws. Clamp the two pieces of wood together with a G-cramp, protecting the faces of the frame pieces with an offcut of wood.

When the adhesive has dried you can drill holes to take reinforcing screws, the heads of which should be countersunk.

To make a cross halving joint use the actual components to mark the crossover point on each. Mark the thickness line, again with a marking gauge, then saw down the lines with a tenon saw.

Place the timber in a vice and chisel out the waste wood. Begin your cut by chiselling out small slivers with the chisel blade held at a slight upward angle, gently tapping the end of the handle.

Repeat for the other side of the joint then remove the pyramid of waste wood gradually from the middle until you have a flat, square-ended joint. Assemble as you would a corner halving joint.

Making the bench top

The bench top is a basic rectangular frame with a cut-out in one long side

to take the barbecue. The entire surface is clad with slats. It's fixed securely to the top of the brickwork unit with screws and plugs.

Cut the inner frame piece to length — it spans the width of the brick unit, plus a 300 mm overhang at each side. It runs along the half-brick connecting wall, resting on a ledge formed on the two single brick walls.

The front frame piece forms the projecting edge of the bench top. It's the same length as the inner piece and is connected to it by four shorter lengths of wood — two outside pieces that form the overhang sides and two inner supporting pieces, which rest on the single brick walls.

All timbers are notched together with halving joints and secured with glue and brass screws, which won't rust. Cut the joints and check that each part fits together accurately.

The entire frame is screwed down to the top of the brick ledge using 100 mm screws and masonry plugs before you add the slatted top to finish off the barbecue unit.

Dry-assemble the frame on a flat surface and make any adjustments. Check that it will fit squarely on top of the brickwork. Before you finally assemble the frame soak all the timber in preservative, paying special attention to the ends and cut-outs. When the preservative has dried, glue and screw the frame together and lift it on top of the brick base. Drill the holes for fixing the frame to the brickwork, mark through them and drill holes in the brickwork for the masonry plugs.

Cut the slats to length and nail or screw them to the frame. Make sure that all nails and screw heads are punched or countersunk below the surface and then fill them with a matching proprietary exterior filler to achieve a neat finish.

Finally, clean up the timberwork, smoothing any sharp or ragged edges with a wood rasp followed by a final sanding with glasspaper.

Apply the finish you've decided on. Set your barbecue onto its shelf and start cooking.

1 Cut all the frame parts to length, joint them and dry assemble

2 Glue and screw the joints of the main frame of the bench top together

3 Drill through the frame and mark the positions of the fixing holes on the bricks. Drill, and screw down

4 Nail the slats to the frame. The small shelves can then be fixed in a similar way using screws and wallplugs

OUTDOOR LIVING

Entertaining out of doors will be much more enjoyable if you make the best use of your garden. An attractive patio and carefully positioned garden lights will help set the scene for your guests. All the information you need is given here, together with practical projects for making your own garden furniture.

GARDEN LIGHTING

Well-designed exterior lighting can turn your patio or garden into a night time wonderland. On warm summer evenings, garden lights enable you to extend your living space outside and make the garden ideal for barbecues and outdoor parties. Even during the winter, when there is frost or snow in the air, exterior lighting adds a sparkling new dimension to the view from your windows.

But exterior lights serve more than just a decorative purpose. You can use them to light up a porch and front door; or to illuminate drives and pathways so that visitors can see the way in. And if street lighting is inadequate, as it often is in rural districts, outdoor lights will illuminate your street number or house name so that visitors can easily find you.

Choosing exterior lights

The variety of exterior lights and lamps almost equals that of interior lighting. Long gone are the days when you could buy only rather crude floodlights which made the garden resemble a football pitch. Modern exterior lights range in function from decorative hanging lanterns to flares which you spike into the grass. Perhaps the most useful way of looking at exterior lights is by showing how and where they can be fixed, since this determines to a large extent how easy or difficult they will be to install.

Wall-mounted lights: The main virtue of lights fixed to a house wall is that they will be easy and cheap to wire up. Several different patterns are available.

The simplest are **porch lights** — in the shape of old-fashioned carriage lanterns, modern globe lights, 'brick' lights, or the more utilitarian bulkhead lights. All these use normal GLS (general lighting

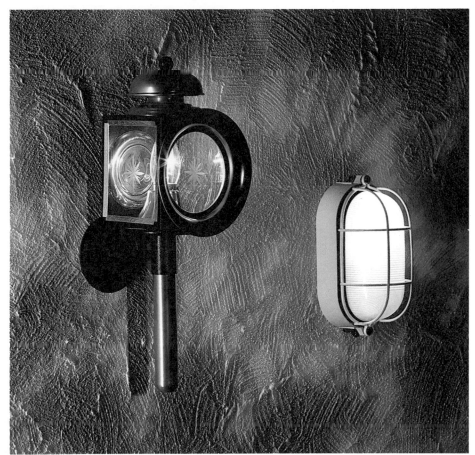

service) bulbs like the ones used in most indoor light fittings. In a clear glass fitting, a 60 W bulb will appear very bright in the dark, and may dazzle; though the light will be softer and easier on the eye if the light has a translucent, diffusing, cover. If you use a porch light on an outside wall, make very certain it is designed for outdoor use; lights marked as *jet-proof* will be, but others should be checked.

Spotlights can be mounted on house walls, too, but it is vital that you get a type which is designed for outdoor use — this will use a PAR (parabolic aluminized reflector) bulb which has a specially-strengthened glass front. It is easy to dazzle people with spotlights, so they are best mounted high up, where they can cover a whole area with light. Note that PAR38 bulbs should be available in both spot and flood versions — the spot type covers a smaller area, but

The careful use of outdoor lights can add a touch of mystery and romance to even the most modest of gardens — just right for parties on summer evenings

gives a more intense light; the flood version will light a larger area but to a lower lighting level.

For the brightest light over a large area, a special **tungsten halogen floodlight** can be used. These are usually mounted high on a building, or on top of a pole, but some types are designed for use at ground level, primarily for floodlighting the side of a building.

All the wall-mounted lights have their place in an outdoor lighting scheme — but if you want the best effects, use them carefully. Flood-lights and the more powerful spot-lights should be kept mainly for utilitarian lighting of drives, paths, yards and so on. But don't forget that patios and barbecue areas need utilitarian lighting too, so that you can see to cook safely. You may well be able to light these areas with some judiciously placed spotlights mounted on house walls. If you can direct the beam through trees or other foliage, to break up the light and provide it with some colour, so much the better.

An alternative trick with spotlights is to mount them low, and shine them up at the house wall — though this may distort the architectural features of the house considerably, it will provide a much softer glow over a particular section of the garden.

Porch lights might provide some of your patio lighting — but be careful to place them where they will not cause glare. The type where the bulb is covered with multi-coloured glass panels might be more restful on the eyes than a clear glass globe — if the style goes well with your house.

Ground-fixed lights: To illuminate parts of your garden away from the house, the safest type of light to use is one that is securely fixed to the ground. One version consists of a steel spike with one or more spotlights mounted on top — you simply drive the spike into the ground wherever you want, and angle the light to illuminate a certain feature (usually a tree, hedge, or shrub). If you change your mind about siting it's easy to pull out the spike and place it somewhere else.

These spotlights are available either as *mains-voltage* or *low-voltage* types. The low-voltage type is based on sealed-beam car head-light lamps; they may be less flexible in beam spread and direction than the mains-voltage types, but they are very much safer and easier to wire (the cable can simply be laid along the ground) and changing their position in the garden is easy. Mains-voltage spotlights can be fitted with a variety of bulbs having different wattages (for varying levels of brightness), beam widths and so on. But wiring them up requires much more care, with the cable being

Spotlights can provide a decorative focus when placed among the shrubbery — push the mounting spike firmly into the ground

buried well underground — and this makes it awkward to move the lights once they have been installed.

Another type of light consists of a totally-enclosed and weatherproof **bollard** with a bulb mounted inside behind a translucent glass or plastic cover. These are part-buried in the ground and can be moved only with some upheaval, so you need to decide carefully first where you want them.

Often, a light mounted at ground level will be all you need in the garden itself — beams aimed upwards at trees and so on will be reflected back to ground level, and bollards, or spotlights aimed downwards, will light the ground sufficiently to make it possible to walk round the garden safely. Remember

that you are not trying to create the levels of lighting that you would need inside the house.

If you do need bright illumination, however, you will have to mount a spotlight up high, and aim its beam down to ground level. Unless you have a sturdy brick wall nearby (in which case you can use any of the wall-mounted lights described above) it is best to use only low-voltage spotlights, for safety. These can be mounted on top of a pole or, for better looks, hidden in the upper branches of a nearby tree.

Festoons (or 'fairy lights') are sets of mains or low-wattage bulbs strung on a flex, and wound (carefully) through trees, along walls and so on. These are mainly for decoration but, of course, provide some illumination for lighting the tree and the surrounding ground as well.

Underwater lights: One of the most spectacular forms of outdoor lighting can be achieved by mounting

To connect mains voltage lights in the garden, drive a post into the ground at the position selected and wire up a 13 amp weatherproof socket

Protect the cable along its run with heavy duty plastic conduit. Bury the cable in a trench at least 500 mm deep

coloured lights in a pond or a fountain. The movement of the water, coupled with the lights, creates a shimmering effect that is quite unique. Needless to say, only special low-voltage completely-sealed lamps must be used in this way. Some types are designed to float on the surface of the water; others can be completely submerged in the pond to shine through the water.

Wiring up

Any exterior light fitting, unless it is sheltered in a porch, must be fully sealed and insulated because it will always be exposed to the elements — even if it is not always switched on. Porch lights and lamps mounted on exterior walls can generally be connected directly into the interior lighting circuit — not always possible with lights distant from the house.

Standard GLS 40 W bulbs — available in many colours — can be fitted to the lampholders of festoon and fairy lights

Use only fittings — lights, sockets, bulbs and so on — that are designed for outdoor use. Unless your lighting circuit is very simple, wire it to a separate fuse on the fuseboard — the circuit should have its own isolating switch as well. In the UK, you could wire a lighting circuit via a fused switched connection unit, fitted to a spur on the right main. Use suitable

WATCHPOINT

Installing an exterior lighting circuit is a job that requires great care — the results must remain safe even after years of exposure to the weather. If you have any doubts about your skills, let a professional do the job.

cable — in the UK, mineral insulated or armoured PVC sheathed, buried at least 500 mm below ground, or ordinary PVC cable protected by heavy-gauge conduit and buried at the same depth.

It is sensible to have the circuit checked by a professional before connecting it (or having it connected for you) to the mains.

Choosing what to illuminate and where to place the lights is almost as critical as selecting the lights themselves. At all times bear in mind that once you have positioned a light outside and buried the cable, repositioning it will be a lengthy job. Always experiment with different locations before you make any final decision — the extra effort will be worthwhile.

Positioning lights

If you simply want to illuminate a drive or pathway, the kind of lights you choose and where you position them will depend mostly on the surroundings. If you have trees lining a sweeping drive or even a narrow path, the lights should be positioned to offer a clear line to the house.

Placing spotlamps up in the trees might add to the interest, but not to the effectiveness of the illumination. And too many lights might also give the drive or path the appearance of an airport runway — it is usually better to keep to as few lights as possible.

A long drive is often adequately served by just one pole-mounted downlighter near the entrance and another closer to the house. Casting a glow over a wide area, these lamps will create a welcoming atmosphere without being excessively obtrusive.

Remember that a powerful single lamp close to the house can serve to illuminate the house itself, so here you might decide that a spot or floodlamp is more effective. Positioned behind a shrub or rockery and pointing upwards to the house, the secret source of light can create a most entrancing and mysterious effect.

Outdoor lighting is essential for evening entertaining, particularly for barbecues and, in a well-appointed patio, there may be separate eating and cooking areas which would best be served by individual lighting of different types.

Powerful spotlamps pointing up towards the house would undoubtedly create too much glare: softer, glowing lamps which cast a more

Flares, which you light with a taper, can be pushed into the ground around the garden. Keep them away from flower beds and tall shrubs

diffused illumination over a wide area would be a better choice. Position one close to the barbecue as this is where you will need the greatest concentration of light.

If there are surrounding walls, they might be the ideal places on which to mount the lights — and spotlamps can be used here sparingly as long as they do not dazzle.

It can be very disconcerting to be confronted by a black gloom just a few feet beyond the patio, so consider adding one or more lights some distance away in the garden. A single lantern in a tree will probably not be enough, particularly in a large area, so experiment carefully with other lights until you achieve a satisfactory compromise for both patio and garden. Inexpensive garden flares can also be bought that can be very effective for lighting up various parts of the garden.

Drawing the eye to one or more points of interest in the garden not only relieves the gloom lying beyond the house, it also enables you to make fuller use of the garden when you are entertaining. Just as lighting a driveway introduces a welcoming atmosphere at the front, so lights in the back garden make it a much friendlier place.

The shape and texture of many natural features in the garden take on quite a different aspect when illu-

minated at night. A lamp, mounted in the trees, creates moving patterns of shadows in the slightest breeze, while spotlamps pick out the delicate tracery of the leaves. Patches of rocks and bricks, shrubs and flowers are all enhanced by illumination: try lighting them from spotlamps hidden away in a tree or bush.

Even from inside the house, especially during the colder months of winter when the trees sparkle with frost or are covered by fingers of snow, the garden itself can become a picture in a window frame.

Illuminated from below by spotlamps, a pergola can be transformed into a night-time roof of greenery; because of the effects of shadows, any foliage thickens and becomes glossy — the very shape and proportion of the garden is often altered beyond recognition at night.

But of all the features in a garden that are transformed by exterior lighting, the most spectacular are pools of water. A fountain or even a pond will sparkle when lit from above by spotlamps or from below by underwater lamps. Plants and ornaments in the water become more distinctive, goldfish shimmer and the contrast with the surrounding shadows is striking.

Lighting the house

The house itself can benefit from some illumination and again spotlamps work best at picking out the most attractive and decorative features.

Lamps mounted on the walls are not generally very effective in this respect because they tend to cast shadows which distort the exterior features.

It is better to position a pair of spotlamps centrally, some distance from the front of the house, so that they can be angled to either side. This ensures that the entire front elevation is evenly illuminated. Alternatively, individual spotlamps can be placed at the sides pointing inwards.

DESIGN A PATIO

A well laid out patio built from attractive purpose made materials will not only be a positive asset to your house but will also be the ideal spot for setting up your barbecue and holding outdoor parties.

You could simply build a patio from slabs of concrete or stone but the chances are that it won't look particularly good or last for very long. This adaptable patio is designed with special clay pavers in mind. They're light and easy to handle, hardwearing and attractive. It's also simple to incorporate matching walls or planters and turn it into a very special feature.

Here we show you how to get your plan down on paper, how to set your patio out so as to avoid costly mistakes, and how to estimate the materials required.

The only tools you will need for the design stage are pencil and paper (preferably graph paper), 300 mm square cut pegs and string for plotting the shape of the patio, a tape measure and a spirit level.

Patio planning

Paper is cheaper than bricks and mortar so it's worthwhile getting the design right before you begin construction.

There are practical problems to be considered as well as visual ones: drainage has to be thought of; the foundations, though not complicated, must be adequate; and you must consider the relationship between the patio, house and garden. Once you have these sorted out, the rest is simply a matter of following the plan through and transferring it onto your site.

Think about location first. Patios are best located where they will catch the sun so it helps if you can give them a south-facing location (in the UK at least). They don't have to be built up against the house wall, but if they are, they are much more likely to become outdoor extensions of your living space. If you already have French windows, you'll want to build up against them for easy access, so the position of your patio will be fixed for you.

Whatever location you are considering for your patio, bear in mind that when it is finished it must have a gradient of 1:40 to channel rainwater away from the building. Provided that your house is sited on level ground, you won't encounter much of a problem as the gradient can be accounted for when you lay the foundations. However, if the ground slopes very steeply away from the house, you can incorporate steps into the design to bring the gradient up to a reasonable level. On the other hand, if there is a slope towards the house, you will have no option but to dig into the bank to accommodate the gradient. This may, of course, involve building a retaining wall to hold back the soil although shallow slopes can be grassed over to stop soil being washed down the slope.

The other hazard you may encounter if you build near the house is a man-hole cover. Do your best to skirt around it and on no account attempt to cover it up — you will only provoke trouble with authorities and potentially cause problems with the drains and have to say goodbye to your patio. If you can't avoid an inspection cover, it may be possible to incorporate a new double-seal cover into your design. You can get these with a recessed top which can be tiled to blend in with the rest of the masonry.

You have a choice when it comes to finishing off the patio paving — it can either be pointed with a 4:1 mix of mortar (rigid paving) or loose-filled with sand (flexible paving). It is largely a matter of personal taste — rigid paving requires less upkeep but tends to look barren, whereas flexible paving looks more informal but attracts weeds.

The gap between flexibly laid pavers is very small — about 2–3 mm — but with rigid paving it is wider, about 10mm. This means that you will probably require more pavers if you decide to use flexible paving (see Choosing and estimating materials).

The size and shape of your patio will depend on what space you have and what you want to use it for. If your garden is tiny, think about turning it all into a patio — every lazy gardener's ambition. If you have no restrictions it is a good idea to build at least one wall as a visual break to the expanse of paving and to act as a wind shield. Try to align new walls with some part of the house or garden to retain visual continuity.

WATCHPOINT

It's best to stick to variations of a rectangle when you design the patio as most building materials are themselves square or rectangular. However, there's no reason why you can't arrange the paving into patterns but it's best to play safe and work them out on paper first.

If you point your slabs, pavers or bricks with mortar you will get a regular, symmetrical pattern often known as rigid paving

By loose-filling your patio flooring material, you will get a more irregular, less rigid effect. This is known as flexible paving and can look very attractive

Even if you don't have to raise the patio to counter a slope that's already there, steps can add to the feature and make it more interesting. If you decide to incorporate steps into the design, play safe and build a shallow wall or planter along the exposed edge — otherwise they can be a safety risk, particularly at night. Each step should not rise more than 175 mm and the tread should not be less than 275 mm deep.

When you have worked out where your patio is going to go, and roughly what features you want to incorporate, make a few trial plans on graph paper. Check back by measuring the actual site to make sure that everything will fit, that it is the right size and that features such as walls and steps line up and are in the right place.

When you are happy with the arrangement go back to the graph paper and make any final adjustments before working out the pattern of the paving in detail. In practice you will be able to make slight adjustments in the position of its parts so that you can avoid cutting bricks or paving. It is important to try and refrain from using cut pavers because apart from looking ugly, they are not easy to chop down to size.

If you are building walls or planters sketch some working drawings so that you can calculate their overall dimensions and work out the coursing of the bricks. The bricks are laid in a simple overlapping pattern called stretcher bond. This is simple to lay and involves few cut bricks. Each course is 75 mm high and you need one brick per 225 mm length.

Use your plans as a basis for estimating, for setting out, and for laying the courses.

Setting out the patio

Armed with your plans you can now start setting out the patio on the ground with string tied to pegs.

It may seem like an unnecessary chore, but if you don't mark out the position of each wall and feature on the ground, you will only end up with an uneven patio. And, provided that you level them properly, the strings can be used to accurately judge the depth of the foundations when it comes to digging them out.

Start by driving two pegs into the ground to mark the corners of the patio nearest the house wall — their tops must be at least 150 mm below the house's damp proof course (DPC). This should be visible as an extra thick line of mortar, about two courses of brickwork above ground.

● Use a spirit level taped to a straight length of timber to check that the tops of the two pegs are level. If necessary, tap one of the pegs in until they are exactly the same height.

● Mark the sides of the patio by knocking in two more pegs directly opposite the first pair but at least 300 mm beyond the outer edge of the patio. Positioning them is easier said than done and you will certainly find it useful to have a large square — a bricklaying square for example — on hand to guarantee that you line them

up correctly. It is the outer faces of the pegs which determine the sides of the patio so when you hammer them in, check that they are square to the walls of the house. Level the pegs before starting to tie the lines between them.

If you have to cope with a slope that falls away from the house, you will need longer pegs in order to get the tops to line up. On the other hand, if you have a slope that comes down to the house, you may have to do a bit of excavating first (see diagram on page 30).

● The lines that mark out the edges of the patio run around the outside of the pegs (see right). In this way the lines — assuming that you have

WATCHPOINT

accurately positioned the pegs — will directly correspond with the perimeter of the patio. As the tops of the pegs are all level with each other, it makes sense to tie the lines as close to the tops as possible.

A basic patio design, which extends the living area out from the house. The space between the planters would be an ideal spot for a barbecue. Bear in mind that a patio with few features will be little more than a barren expanse of paving

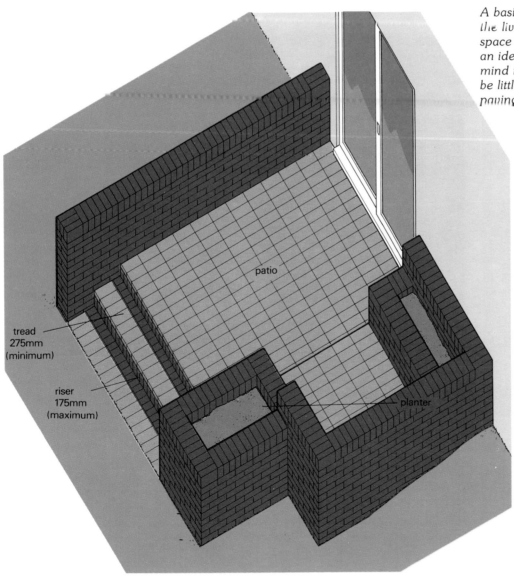

tread 275mm (minimum)

riser 175mm (maximum)

patio

planter

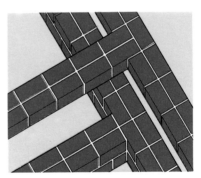

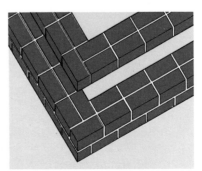

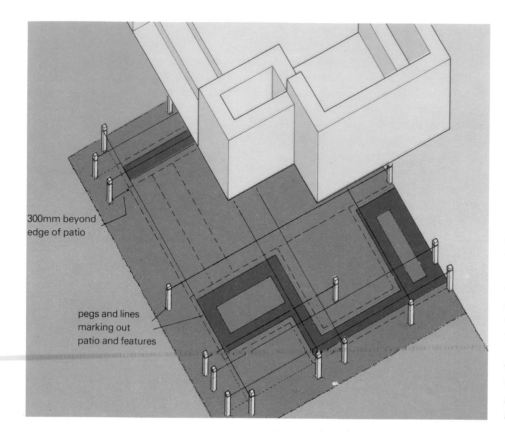

300mm beyond
edge of patio

pegs and lines
marking out
patio and features

Plot out the shape of the patio and its features using lines tied around pegs — each line must correspond to an extreme edge of either the patio itself or a feature

Choosing and estimating the materials

When deciding which materials to choose for your patio, bear in mind the following considerations.

Paving: You can make a patio from concrete slabs, bricks or even timber sleepers but for ease of building, durability and appearance, purpose made clay pavers are the best option. They vary in size according to the type of paving — thicker ones are used for flexible paving — and are available in a wide variety of colours and textures.

1 Mark out the patio position using wooden pegs. Position 300 mm beyond edge of patio

2 Provided that the pegs aren't too far apart, check horizontal alignment with a spirit level

3 Tie the lines in such a way that they are level with the tops of the pegs. A nail at an angle will hold the line

It's easier to fiddle about with pegs at this stage than to trim pavers later on so take your time to get the lines straight.
● In the same fashion set up pegs and lines for the walls running parallel to the house — but remember to keep the pegs outside the perimeter of the patio.

● When all the features — including planters and steps — have been delineated, make sure that everything is square by checking the diagonals. If it is square, the diagonals will be the same. When you are satisfied, you are all set to start digging the foundations. Dimensions for these are given on page 31.

WATCHPOINT

Tying the lines around the tops of the pegs is made much easier if you hammer the nails into the tops first. You can then bend the nails over in order to trap the lines in place.

Features: Manufacturers of pavers usually also make a wide range of bricks from which you can make walls and planters so you shouldn't have any trouble in finding some to match the walls of your house. It's important to buy special engineering bricks that are resistant to frost — which is not always the case with second hand ones from demolition contractors.

Foundations: The base layer is made up of 100 mm of hardcore. You can either buy hardcore or make up your own from rubble and old broken bricks — provided that the bits are broken into pieces no larger than 50 mm across.

The second layer consists of 100 mm of concrete mixed in the ratio of 15 parts all in-ballast to 1 part ordinary Portland cement.

The bedding layer varies in thickness according to how you choose to lay the paving: 30 mm of mortar for rigid paving, 50 mm of sand for flexible paving.

Pointing: For flexible paving all you require is fine sharp sand to fill the gaps between pavers. For rigid paving you will need a 4:1 mix of mortar. When bricklaying (building walls and planters) you will need a standard mix of 4 parts soft sand to 1 part cement.

Working out the quantities

There is no easy way of estimating but it makes sense to buy the paving and bricks by number and the foundation materials by volume.

To work out how many pavers you will need, calculate the total area of the patio in square metres and then multiply this figure by the number of pavers that fit into one square metre — 45 for flexible paving or 40 for rigid. Always allow 5 per cent extra for cutting and wastage.

Calculating the number of bricks you need for the walls is slightly more

WATCHPOINT

Pavers are usually sold by the pallet load of 400 and it costs proportionately more if you have to buy odd quantities. So, if possible, buy complete loads. And remember that it is the haulage which may add very considerably to the cost so make sure that you order all you want in one go.

complicated because there are likely to be so many small sections. Measure each of these and add the areas together. You need 120 bricks to build 1 square metre of wall so multiply that figure by the total area. If you are in doubt, ask your supplier

It is a mistake to construct a plain patio without features. Planters, retaining walls and steps all add interest

for help: they make such calculations every day.

Alternatively, draw out a plan for each section of wall. You will find that you only need to work out the first two courses; you can then estimate the rest.

For the foundation materials, you will have to calculate the volume of each layer — the area multiplied by the thickness — before you can buy the appropriate quantities of sand, cement and aggregate. If your dealer sells the material by weight, he will be able to help you make the necessary conversions.

SIMPLE PATIO TABLE

and cedar of Lebanon. Durable hardwoods either originate in tropical Africa, South America, south-east Asia or Europe. The first group includes teak, afrormosia, iroko, makore and utile. The latter includes such traditionally durable woods as elm, oak and beech.

Nearly all man-made boards are destroyed by the first hint of damp, the only certain exception being 'marine' grade ply. Even EXT (exterior), BR (boil resistant) and WBP (weather and boil proof) grade plywoods should be used with caution. Moreover, plywood may pose an aesthetic problem in the natural surroundings of a garden,

The design relies for strength more on sound construction principles than on complicated woodworking joints, so most of the parts simply screw and glue together. You do have to make two mortise and tenon joints on the centre rail, but thanks to the rustic nature of the table it's not essential that these are completely accurate. In fact, if you haven't done much woodworking before, this is an excellent introduction to the art.

Tools and materials

The materials that you will need are straight-forward. They consist of:
● 9.7 m of 100 mm × 25 mm tongued-and-grooved pine floorboarding from which to cut eight lengths to 1200 mm.
● 4.9 m of 100 × 25 mm PAR softwood from which to cut the centre rail to 110 mm and the four legs to approximately 900 mm.
● 1.8 m of 50 mm × 50 mm PAR softwood from which to cut 4 tabletop braces to a length of 450 mm.

You also require eight 62 mm No. 8 and sixteen 38 mm No. 8 countersunk woodscrews for the fixings. As these will almost certainly be exposed to moisture, make sure that they're stainless steel, brass,

The essence of garden and patio furniture is that it should be simple yet sturdy. This table fulfils both requirements admirably, combining rustic good looks with a construction method so simple that even the least confident of carpenters should have no trouble building it themselves in just a few hours.

The basic material is PAR (planed-all-round) softwood, which means that you have plenty of choice when it comes to finish — choose from paint, varnish, or stain, according to the surroundings. And all the sizes are standard, so there should be no problems with availability. It's worth buying preservative-treated timber, or else treating untreated wood with

The perfect item for meals outdoors or drinks on the patio, this table can be easily dismantled for storage

a clear preservative before assembly, to keep rot at bay. In order to obtain long-lasting results, you should follow the manufacturer's instructions carefully. Be warned, however, as the treatment tends to be lengthy and messy.

Nearly all hardwoods have to be preserved too. There are, however, several types of timber that will withstand the vagaries of inclement weather without requiring any special treatment.

Weather-resistant softwoods include yew, larch, western red cedar galvanized or black japanned. For the same reason, your woodworking glue must be a waterproof urea or resorcinol formaldehyde resin type — ask for 'exterior woodworking glue'. Resorcinol (formaldehyde) is by far the stronger of the two.

When it comes to tools, your prime requirement is a good sharp panel saw to cut the timber. It's well worth checking the blade on yours before you start the job: if it feels dull and fails to catch the skin when you run it across your hand, it is almost certainly blunt. Find a hardware store or tool supplier offering a sharpening service; it's worth the effort, and the charges are a lot less than the cost of a new saw.

The rest of the tools should present no problems: you'll need a tape measure, try square, sliding bevel and marking knife for measuring; a drill, twist bits and screwdriver for fixing; a planer file, sanding block and abrasive paper for finishing; and a 25 mm woodworking chisel and padsaw for cutting the mortises. A tenon saw, mitre block and pairs of sash and G-cramps will all come in handy but they are not essential providing you have a workbench incorporating a vice or clamping facility.

Making the table top

This is simple. Accurate cutting and a little improvisation with the cramping should guarantee perfect results.

Start by sawing the tongued-and-grooved boards to length. Measure the first length using a tape measure and mark a line across it using your try square. When you saw it, take care to keep the blade to the waste side of the line so that the rough edge can be trimmed later.

Use the cut length as a template to measure the rest so that you avoid cumulative errors. Rather than being tempted to cut one length after the other, leave a little waste wood between each one so that you avoid

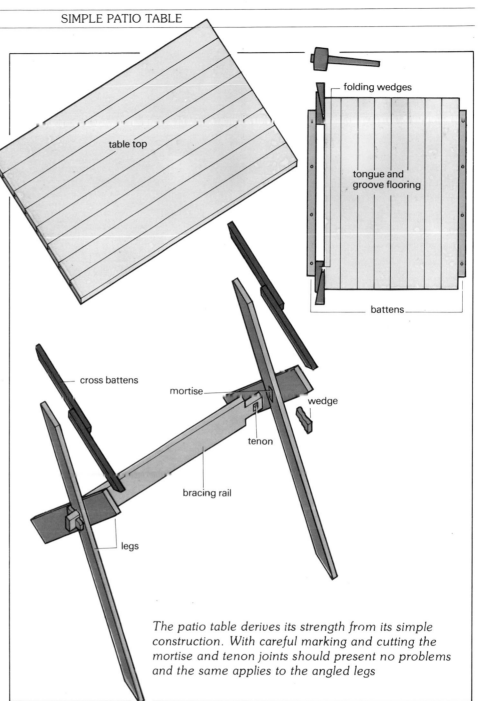

The patio table derives its strength from its simple construction. With careful marking and cutting the mortise and tenon joints should present no problems and the same applies to the angled legs

possible inaccuracies on the previous cut: it means more sawing, but it ensures that all the boards are the same length.

The edge board on one side of the top will be left with an exposed tongue, while that on the other will have the groove exposed. So before you go any further, carefully saw the tongue off one of the lengths, keeping the blade hard against the full edge. Alternatively, use a plane. You'll need this (or a planer file) to remove the groove from the edge of

another length. Check with your try square that each edge is planed square along its entire length and remedy discrepancies with your plane and glasspaper.

To assemble the table top, the boards must be securely clamped. And unless you own a pair of sash cramps, you'll need a wood floor on which to improvise a simple, but very effective cramping jig.

Make the jig by screwing two 1 m lengths of 50 mm × 25 mm batten to the floor. The battens must be exactly parallel to one another, and about 825 mm apart (that is, the width of the table top plus a bit more). Use more offcuts of the same timber to cut two pairs of 'folding' wedges about 150 mm long, as shown in the diagram on page 33.

If the floor surface between the jig battens isn't perfectly flat, cut a piece of hardboard or similar material to size and lay it between them or, better still, position the hardboard first and screw the battens to the floor through it. That way, the wood will not slip or bow in any way.

Take one of the edge boards, apply glue along the mating edge, and lay it in the jig against the far batten. Glue up the next board and slot it against the first one, checking as you do so that the ends are exactly square. Continue in this way until all eight boards are in place in the jig and then check again that the ends are square by holding a straightedge against them.

You can now clamp the boards by driving in the folding wedges between the last edge board and the nearest batten. Don't force the wedges or the boards may buckle: they're tight enough when you can't extract them by hand. Wipe away spilt or excess glue with a damp cloth before it dries.

Inspect the boards ends closely to ensure that they are all lying flat and that the tongues are fully engaged. Then lay a flat board and a few weights on top of the table boards and leave the entire assembly to dry.

In the meantime, cut the four cross braces to length: as before, use the first as a template to measure and mark the other three. The ends of the braces must be bevelled by making 45° mitre cuts. If you don't have a mitre box or block to guide you, mark the mitres with a sliding bevel and square lines across the adjoining edges of the wood so that you have guides by which to keep the saw blade vertical. After cutting, sand the rough edges lightly with a planer file or coarse glasspaper.

When the top is made, you can

1 Measure and cut the first length of tongued-and-grooved board, then use it as a template to mark up and cut the others

move onto making the base. Don't disturb the top until you're quite sure the glue is dry or you may knock the boards out of alignment.

Making the base

This looks more difficult than it is. The angled cuts on the legs are in fact straightforward mitres, and if you measure up carefully you will have no trouble getting the table to sit squarely. Cutting the mortises is covered separately.

Start with the legs. As with the top boards, you measure and cut the first one to size and then use this to measure and mark the others. Take as much care and time as you need to ensure that all the legs will be the same length. There are few things as annoying or unsightly as a table that leans to one side or rocks every time you put something on it.

The distance between the mitres is 832 mm, so begin by marking this off along one edge of the timber. Set your sliding bevel to 45° and mark the mitres across the board, noting that they both run in the same direction. Then use your square to draw lines across the edge to act as vertical cutting guides.

Clamp the timber firmly before

2 Mark a 45° mitre on the outside end of the four cross braces with a sliding bevel, then mark square lines across the adjoining edges

sawing. Take care to keep the blade vertical at all times and to cut to the waste side of the lines. It's surprising just how many aspiring woodworkers face disappointment through failing to appreciate that just the width of their saw blade is sufficient to put their work completely out of true. Sand the cut edges lightly — just enough to remove any roughness.

With the first leg cut, mark off the others. Use a marking knife — it's more accurate than a pencil.

Sort the cut legs into pairs. Take the first pair, arrange them into an X shape as they will be fixed, and lay the ends against a wall or straight-edged board. Bring up another board against the other ends and adjust the X until all the ends lie flat against the surfaces they are pushed against.

At this point, the X should be square, but you can check by laying your try square in the angles made by the boards where they cross — they should all be 90°.

Prop the boards in this position so that there is no danger of them slipping and drill four pilot holes around the intersection as shown in step 7. Take care not to drill right through the lower board — use a depth stop to prevent this from happening.

Now work out which board will be on the inside in the finished construc-

3 Having cut the first leg, use it as a template to mark up the others. Use a knife, which is more accurate than a pencil

4 Holding the legs in an X shape against two flat surfaces, test the accuracy of the mitres by checking that they cross at right angles

5 Mark the centre of the legs, then drill four clearance holes and countersinks on the inside face of both of the inside legs

6 Mark the tenons on the cross brace rail using either a marking gauge or, providing the ends are square, a try square

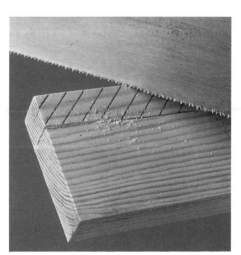

7 Remove the waste with four cuts, using a tenon saw if you have one; make sure that the work is well clamped-up first

8 With the base assembled tap the wedges in gently until they're locked and the legs sit squarely against the bracing rail tenons

WATCHPOINT

Don't assume that the ends of the timber are square: square your own lines and cut both ends to waste wood.

tion — this is the one you screw through. Ensure that you have the right face uppermost, drill clearance holes and countersinks for 38 mm screws through the pilot holes. Finally, apply glue to the mating surfaces and screw the two legs together. Repeat this procedure for the other pair of legs. Wipe away any excess glue straight away with a damp cloth before it sets.

Cut the bracing rail to length, ensuring that both ends are absolutely square.

Mark the tenons on the rail according to the dimensions on the diagram. You can use a marking gauge if you have one, but providing the ends are square it's just as easy to mark each line individually using your try square. Extend all the lines over to the edges of the board, to give yourself cutting guides, and cross-hatch the waste wood in pencil so that there's no confusion later on over what needs to be removed.

The waste can be removed with four saw cuts. Use a tenon saw if you have one, otherwise use your panel saw and make certain that the timber is firmly clamped. As always, cut to the waste side of the lines and use the edge lines to keep the blade vertical. After sawing, remove any roughness by sanding the cut ends lightly.

Complete this stage of the job by marking and cutting the mortises in

9 Having drilled and countersunk the clearance holes in the cross braces, glue and screw them firmly to the table top

the leg assemblies and bracing rail tenons as described in Cutting the mortises. Then you can prepare for the final assembly.

Assembly

Don't embark on assembly until you are sure that the table top is dry. Start by reassembling the base — without glue — so that you can use it as a guide to accurately positioning the necessary cross braces.

Cut the wedges which lock the bracing rail from an offcut of 50 mm × 25 mm softwood. The shape isn't critical, but you must ensure that they are larger than 25 mm square at the thick end; you'll get a more authentic effect if you saw them roughly to size and then do the final shaping with a handyman's knife or rasp. Tap the wedges in gently until they're locked and the legs sit squarely against the shoulders of the bracing rail tenons.

Lay the table top upper face downwards and place the assembled base on top. Adjust the position of the base until it sits squarely within the top — that is, when corresponding measurements taken from the edge to the legs are equal on both sides.

Now position the cross braces hard

against the legs as shown in the picture on page 33 and adjust so that the bevelled ends are flush with the edge of the top. Without disturbing any of the components, drill holes through the braces into the top at 100 mm centres; mark the bit with

WATCHPOINT

If you decide on varnish, use an exterior grade. If you paint the table, give it a base coat of primer/undercoat followed by two of gloss paint. But better than both of these finishes is a preservative wood stain.

tape as a depth gauge to avoid drilling right through the table top as you do this.

Remove the cross braces and convert the pilot holes into countersunk clearance holes. Apply glue to the mating surfaces, then screw the braces firmly to the top.

The final assembly job is to screw the ends of the legs to the braces. Depending on the size of your drill, you can either position the legs and drill pilot holes straight through or else measure up and drill everything separately.

Give the entire table a thorough sanding with fine grade paper mounted on a block prior to applying your chosen finish.

Cutting the mortises

All the mortises in this project are through mortises, so cutting them is straightforward. The difficulty is in getting them in the right place, so that all the parts line up.

Start with the leg mortises. The bracing rail is too large for direct measuring, so your first job is to cut a cardboard template to the exact size of the tenons. Measure and mark a cross in the centre of this as shown in the illustration.

Set the two leg assemblies exactly

on top of one another and prop them in this position. Now square a cross in the centre of the intersection.

Lay the template over the cross so that the two crosses align and mark around the outside to give the exact position of the mortise.

Keeping the leg assemblies together, drill pilot holes right through all the timber at each corner of the mortise; take great care to ensure that the holes are within the marked lines, and drill through into scrap wood.

Separate the leg assemblies for cutting. If you have a keyhole or coping saw, insert the blade in the pilot holes to cut out the bulk of the waste, then trim with a chisel. Otherwise, drill joined-up holes right around the mortise, knock out the waste, then trim.

Assemble the legs and bracing rail in a dry run to test the fit. Assuming all is well, strike off a line on each tenon against the legs to mark the position of the wedge mortises. It is then a simple matter to dismantle the rail and mark the remaining three sides (the mortises are 25 mm square).

Cut the mortises in the same way as you did those on the legs.

Choosing a finish

Painting: This must be carried out thoroughly if the finish is to last. This means using a primer, undercoat and at least two top coats, and paying particular attention to edges, corners and endgrain.
Varnishing: This also requires similar care in application, and for long-lasting results it's better to use a resin varnish than a polyurethane one.
Staining: This can be carried out with ordinary woodstains that are then varnished over, but a longer-lasting result will be achieved with a preservative stain; this colours and preserves the wood without forming a surface film, so there's no risk of peeling.

PICNIC TABLE & BENCHES

Many of the picnic tables and benches that are in the stores incorporate their benches in one large assembly and consequently they're difficult to clamber over to sit down, and they can't be taken apart quickly or easily for storage during bad weather or the winter. This attractive garden set, however, has two separate benches and the table has folding legs so that it can be stacked out of the way in a shed or garage when it's not needed. It's simple to set up and easy to make.

Only basic woodworking skills are needed to make the table and benches, because all the joints are glued and pinned together. The table shown measures 1495 mm × 750 mm and the benches 1195 mm × 400 mm, but you can alter the sizes to suit your needs.

Materials

Since the table and benches will spend a lot of time outside, use a hardwood such as beech or elm — this will last longer than a softwood like pine, although it will cost more. All the timber sizes given below are nominal so you may find slight variations.

The table battens are cut from 100 mm × 25 mm PAR (planed-all-round) timber. You'll need enough wood for the following pieces:
- Fifteen 750 mm lengths for the top battens (A in Fig. A shown on page 38).
- Two 1495 mm lengths for the side rails (B).
- Two 706 mm lengths for the top crossmembers (C).
- Four 765 mm lengths for the legs (D).
- Two 704 mm lengths for the horizontal leg braces (E).
- Four 456 mm lengths for the legs' folding braces (F).
- Two 750 mm lengths of 25 mm dowel (G).

- Two 704 mm lengths of 25 mm dowel (H).
- Two 658 mm lengths of 25 mm dowel (I).
- Two 125 mm lengths of 75 mm × 38 mm batten and two 125 mm lengths of 75 mm × 50 mm batten for the leg clamps (J).
- Two 100 mm long, 6 mm diameter coach bolts with matching wingnuts.
- Eight 50 mm chromed No. 8 countersunk woodscrews.
The benches are made from 75 mm × 25 mm PAR timber throughout and for two you'll need the following:
- Thirty-two 400 mm lengths for the top battens (U).
- Four 1195 mm lengths for the top rails (V).
- Four 356 mm lengths for the horizontal crossmembers (W).

This easily-made folding table and bench set will provide attractive seating for your guests

- Eight 702 mm lengths for the legs (X).
- Four 400 mm lengths for the horizontal leg braces (Y).
- Eight 410 mm lengths for the diagonal leg braces (Z).

In addition to the above materials, you'll need a supply of 18 mm and 38 mm sherardized oval nails, some waterproof wood glue, some clear wood preservative and good-quality exterior varnish.

Tools

A basic woodworking took kit is all that is needed to make both the table

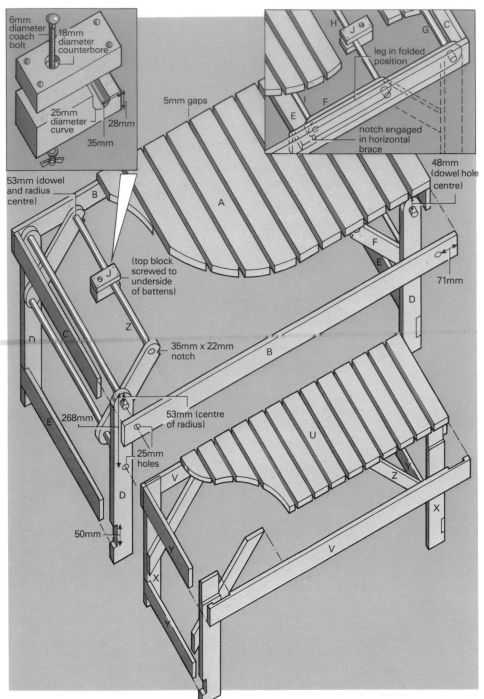

Figure labels within the illustration:

6mm diameter coach bolt
18mm diameter counterbore
25mm diameter curve
28mm
35mm
53mm (dowel and radius centre)
5mm gaps
leg in folded position
notch engaged in horizontal brace
48mm (dowel hole centre)
(top block screwed to underside of battens)
35mm x 22mm notch
71mm
53mm (centre of radius)
268mm
25mm holes
50mm

cal components roughly to length, cramp them all together, and saw or shape them in one operation. Similarly, the holes for the 25 mm dowels should be drilled through matching pieces in one operation to ensure perfect alignment. By working in this way, you will only have to mark out one piece of each set as a template and you will be certain that each of the components is the same size.

The table

With the exception of the 25 mm dowels and the blocks for the leg clamps (see Making and positioning the clamps), the entire table is made from 100 mm × 25 mm PAR timber. All the pieces can be cut to their exact dimensions at this stage, apart from the legs and braces which should be cut oversize so that their ends can be rounded off. You may wish to leave cutting the top battens (A) until the supporting framework is made to ensure that they fit properly (each should be 750 mm long). If you're building a table to the dimensions shown you'll need fifteen of them.

Cut two 706 mm top crossmembers (C) and two 1495 mm side rails (B), leaving the latter cramped together after cutting. Using a marking gauge, scribe the centre line on the face of one rail and make a mark on this line 71 mm in from each end. Drill a 25 mm diameter hole through both pieces at each mark and then widen the holes with a half-round file so that a length of 25 mm dowel will turn freely in them. If you don't have a half-round file to enlarge the holes with, you can always taper the ends of the dowels that will slot into the holes instead. In many ways this is easier than filing down the sides of the holes, provided you use a fine glasspaper and follow the grain of the wood. Try not to exaggerate the taper or else there will be unsightly gaps.

Cut two 704 mm lengths of batten

and benches. It should include a marking gauge, 18 mm and 25 mm bevel-edge chisels, a selection of wood bits, an electric drill and a half-round file. A pair of sash cramps and four small G-cramps are essential for holding the pieces together during construction — if you don't possess these, you can hire them cheaply from your local tool hire shop.

When cutting out the parts for the table and benches, remember to

All the rigid joints of the table are reinforced with adhesive and 38 mm nails. The benches are held firm with diagonal nails

square all the cutting lines around each piece with your try square and score along each line with a marking knife so that the wood won't splinter when you start sawing.

In most instances it will simplify matters if you cut groups of identi-

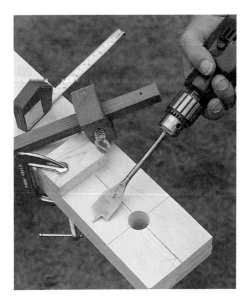

1 Leave the side rails clamped together after cutting and drill 25 mm dowel holes through both rails

2 Enlarge the holes slightly with a half-round file so that the dowels will be able to rotate freely

3 Using compasses scribe an arc at the top of each leg and cut out the waste with a coping saw

for the horizontal leg braces (E) and four 765 mm lengths for the legs themselves (D). Score the centre line on the face of one leg and mark off along it at 48 mm, 53 mm and 268 mm intervals from one end.

Set your compass point on the 53 mm mark and scribe an arc from one end of the batten to the other. This represents the curved top of the leg. Now measure 715 mm along the centre line from the point where it is cut by the arc and square a line across the face of the batten — this is the bottom of the leg. Measure back along the centre line from this point 50 mm, align your try square with the mark, and square a line across the leg. Take a piece of scrap 100 mm × 25 mm batten and stand it on the leg so that its edge is aligned with the line you have just drawn and its face is flush with the edge of the leg. Draw round the offcut to transfer its profile to the leg. This will be the cutout for the horizontal leg brace.

Cramp the leg battens together and square the bottom line around all four. Similarly, mark the brace cutout lines across the leg edges and on to the face of the outer leg. As before, use the scrap piece to mark the exact profile.

Using a tenon saw, cut right

through all four legs at the bottom, taking care to keep to the waste side of your cutting line. When you saw through the edges of the legs to the bottom of the brace cutouts, make several cuts through the waste portion to make removal easier.

Drill 25 mm diameter holes through all four legs at the 48 mm and 268 mm marks and open out the lower one with your half-round file so that a 25 mm dowel will turn freely in it. Chisel the waste from the brace cutouts, using a 25 mm bevel-edged chisel and working in from each side towards the centre. Check that the horizontal braces fit snugly in the cutouts.

Round off the top of each leg separately with a jigsaw or coping saw, making sure that you keep the blade vertical all the time.

Now for the folding leg braces (F). First cut four 456 mm lengths of batten and mark the centre line on the face of one. Mark off along the centre line 53 mm from one end and then 31 mm from this first mark. These two points represent the centres for the supporting dowels and also the radii of the shaped ends. Set your marking gauge to the thickness of the wood you are using and scribe a short line, parallel with

the edge of the batten, so that it cuts through the arc at one end and finishes in line with a dowel centre. Mark off along the centre line 35 mm from where it is cut by the arc, and square a line across the batten. The two lines describe the notch that has to be cut out to make way for the horizontal leg brace when the legs are folded up.

Cramp the battens together and drill 25 mm holes through all four at the points marked. Shape the ends of the braces like the tops of the legs. Having rounded the ends, transfer the outline of the notches across the edges of the battens and on to the remaining exposed side. Cut out the waste with a tenon saw.

The remaining pieces for the table are the 25 mm dowels; cut two 750 mm lengths (G), two 704 mm and two 658 mm lengths (H) and (I).

The benches

The method of marking out and cutting the components for the benches is very similar to that of the table but all the timber is 75 mm × 25 mm PAR.

The top of each bench is made

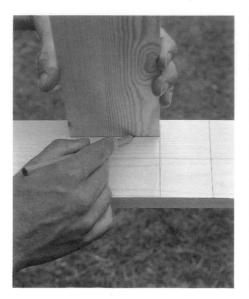

4 Mark the horizontal brace cutouts on the legs using an offcut as a guide

5 Having rounded off the ends of the braces, saw out the notches

6 Halving joints are used to connect the legs to the bench side rails

from 16 battens (U), each 400 mm long. These are supported on a frame of two 1195 mm rails (V) with a 356 mm crossmember (W) positioned at each end.

The two outer rails must be cut with halving joints to accept the tops of the 420 mm long bench legs. Taking each corner in turn, lay a rail down flat and stand a crossmember on top so that it is flush with the end. Mark the rail by running a pencil across the inner face of the cross-member. Then lay a leg on the rail with one edge against the pencil line and mark both rail and leg where each is overlapped by the other.

Set your marking gauge to half the thickness of the wood and score the joint depth on the edges of each piece. Square the face lines down the edges to meet these marks. Cut out the waste with a tenon saw and 25 mm bevel-edged chisel, working in from each edge towards the centre to avoid splintering.

The legs are strengthened by two 400 mm horizontal braces (Y) which are let into the legs in the same manner as the table, and four diagonal braces (Z) measuring 410 mm long. The ends of the diagonal braces are mitred at 45° — if you don't have a mitre box wide

enough to accept the batten, set a sliding bevel to 45° and use this to mark the angled cutting line.

When you have sawn all the pieces to length, clean up the rough edges and remove any pencil marks with some fine glasspaper wrapped round a wooden sanding block.

Before assembling the table and benches, treat all the pieces with two coats of clear wood preservative.

Assembly

Assembling the table and benches is straight-forward as all the components are just nailed and glued together. Use sash cramps to hold the frames rigid until the glue sets.

Construct the table and benches on a level uncluttered surface so that as each frame is made, it can be put aside and laid down flat while the glue dries.

Table assembly

The design of the table is such that the various components must be put together in a specific sequence.

Begin with the folding leg braces, followed by the leg assemblies, then the table-top frame. Finish off by fitting the table-top battens and the leg clamps (see Making the clamps).

Assemble each of the folding braces in a dry run before you start gluing the pieces together. Start by connecting two 456 mm battens together with a 658 mm length of dowel. Slot the dowel through the holes nearest the notches — the ends of the dowel must be flush with the outer faces. Slide a 704 mm length of dowel through the other pair of holes, and, with the battens parallel with each other, check that this dowel protrudes by an equal amount at each end. Measure the diagonals to check that the frame is square and then run a pencil around the top dowel on the inside of the side battens, and around the lower dowel on each side of the battens.

Dismantle the frame and spread glue on the ends of the dowels between the pencil marks. Then reassemble the frame, wipe off any excess glue with a damp cloth, and set it aside on a flat surface for the glue to dry.

Once you have made the two braces, start on the leg assemblies. Dealing with one pair at a time, slot

40

7 Set a sliding bevel to 45° and use it to mark the mitres on the braces

8 Use an offcut to ensure that the dowel protrudes by the correct amount

9 Complete the brace assembly and push the legs onto the dowel ends

the protruding dowels of a brace into the appropriate holes in the legs.

Insert the remaining 704 mm length of dowel through the top leg holes so that they protrude by an equal amount on each side. Mark the top dowel for gluing as before.

Apply glue to the top dowel and the horizontal brace cutouts and assemble the components as shown. Secure the horizontal brace at each end with two 38 mm oval nails. Use a nail punch to sink the nail heads below the surface of the wood. Check that the framework is square and pin a scrap batten across the top to hold it while the glue sets.

Having allowed the leg assemblies to dry, move on to the top frame. Glue the two crossmembers to one of the side rails, reinforcing each joint with a pair of 38 mm nails. Set this assembly on a flat surface, with the crossmembers uppermost, and fit

WATCHPOINT

If the dowels stick, try rubbing some candle wax on the insides of the holes — this will lubricate the dowels and allow them to rotate smoothly.

each leg assembly into its hole in the side rail — make sure the folding brace of each can open inwards towards the centre of the table. Apply glue to the exposed ends of the crossmembers and fit the remaining side rail, taking care to locate the free ends of the leg dowels as you do so. Pin the side rail as before and fit sash cramps until the glue dries.

Glue and pin the top battens to the frame spacing them at 5 mm intervals and using 38 mm nails punched below the surface.

The final job, before applying two coats of varnish, is to fit the leg clamps to the table.

Making the clamps

Each table leg assembly is held in the open and folded positions by a wooden clamp screwed to the underside of the table top. Each clamp is made from two 125 mm long blocks of wood; one cut from 75 mm × 38 mm PAR batten and the other from 75 mm × 50 mm batten. The thinner of the two sections is screwed to the underside of the table top and has a bolt passing

through it which secures the lower section with a wing nut and washer. This part of the clamp fits over the leg brace dowels.

Having cut the wood to size for one clamp, mark the centre line on the face of the upper block and make a mark on this line 30 mm in from one end. With the two pieces clamped together, use an 18 mm flat wood bit to bore a hole in the top block at the point marked to a depth of about 6 mm. This will act as a counterbore for the bolt head. Then drill a 6 mm diameter hole through the centre of this and right through both blocks.

Separate the two blocks and drill a 4.5 mm diameter screw clearance hole at each corner of the upper block. Countersink these on the lower face.

To shape the cutout for the leg braces, secure the lower half of the clamp on its side in a vice and drill a 25 mm diameter hole down through the wood. The centre of the hole must be 35 mm from the end furthest from the bolt hole and 12.5 mm down from the upper face. Great care is needed to keep the bit running vertically — if you have one, use a vertical drill stand. If you don't have a drill stand, stand a try square on edge

10 The top side rails are the last pieces to go on. Check that the braces swivel

11 Finish off the table frame by fixing the rails to the crossmembers

12 Fix the top battens to the bench frame before adding the legs

next to the drill and use it as a visual guide to keeping the bit vertical.

Set your marking gauge to 28 mm and, with its stop against the lower face of the block, mark a cutting line from the 25 mm hole along the edge, across the end grain and along the opposite edge back to the hole. Square another cutting line from the inner edge of the hole on one side, across the upper face and down to the inner edge of the hole on the other side. Cut out the waste with a tenon saw to achieve the shape shown.

Insert the coach bolt through the hole in the upper block and hammer its head down into the counterbore so that its square shank bites into the wood.

Loosely assemble each clamp, turn the table upside down and position the clamps centrally under the top battens.

Open out the table legs so that they are vertical and set the clamps so that they hold the braces in position, clasping the upper dowel. Then, without disturbing the clamps, disengage the braces and fold the legs into the table top — the clamps should engage the lower dowels. Adjust the setting of the clamps and mark their positions.

Remove and dismantle the clamps, set the upper blocks back in place and mark the screw holes on

the underside of the top battens. Make a pilot hole at each point with a bradawl and screw the blocks to the table with 50 mm No. 8 countersunk screws.

If you use brass screws, first cut the thread in each hole with a steel screw of the same size; brass screws are quite soft and will often snap in half if used to cut their own threads.

Finishing the table

Once you have fixed both the clamps to the underside of the top battens, try opening and closing the legs — you may find that on one pair of legs, the horizontal dowel doesn't engage cleanly in its clamp cutout. If this is the case, don't despair as the simple remedy is to enlarge the bolt hole in the lower half of the clamp into a slot. If you do this, you will be able to slide the block along so that it can cope with variations in dowel positions.

If you have to make a slot, leave the block attached to the table while you accurately measure up and mark the exact length you want the slot to be. Then remove the lower block by unscrewing the wingnut and hold it secure in a vice or in the jaws of an adjustable workbench.

Drill a series of 6 mm holes inside the slot outline, making absolutely

sure that you keep the drill vertical all the time. Cut out the waste wood between the 6 mm holes using a coping saw or fine padsaw. Smooth down the sides of the slot with a strip of glasspaper.

Reassemble the clamp and test its operation on the table once more.

You may also find a similar discrepancy in one of the folding leg braces when it is in its folded position — the 35 mm × 22 mm notch may not be long enough to engage the horizontal brace fully. Again, this is easy to put right by increasing the width or depth of the notch with a tenon saw. Be sure to mark and square up cutting lines with a pencil and try square.

Bench assembly

Pin and glue the side rails and crossmembers in the same manner as the table. When the glue has set add the top battens, spacing them at 6 mm intervals. Don't forget to sink the nailheads well below the surface.

Attach the legs to the side rails with glue, reinforcing each joint with four 18 mm nails. Fit the horizontal leg braces across the bottom of each pair of legs, and then glue and nail the diagonal braces between the legs and the top rails. Finish off with varnish.

BARBECUE RECIPES

Barbecue food ranges from the simple to the sophisticated — it all tastes good when cooked out of doors. Fill the evening air with delicious aromas when you cook our barbecue recipes — among them Spicy Chicken, Dindings Duck, Stilton Steak, Bacon Kebabs and Tandoori Fish. To accompany these main courses there are starters, salads and summer drinks.

PREPARING BARBECUE FOOD

Charcoal-grilled food — cooked and served out of doors — is guaranteed to make a success of any social gathering; not only is the air filled with the delicious aromas that come from the fire, but the informality of the occasion — plus the fact that one or two guests always seem to enjoy a turn at the grill — makes for a relaxed party atmosphere.

The choice of food that can be cooked on the barbecue is virtually unlimited, ranging from fruit and vegetables to meat, fish and poultry. One of the beauties of barbecuing is that sometimes the food can be very simple: a beach barbecue, for instance calls for grilled fish, sausages or burgers — seasoned only with salt, lemon and herbs — and the tang of the sea air! But some occasions require food which is a little more sophisticated, and when the kitchen and store cupboard is at hand there is no reason not to experiment with marinades and basting sauces — which can be made with very little effort, once you have bought the basic ingredients.

Working out your menu a day or two in advance, and observing a few simple rules about cooking on charcoal, will guarantee tempting food — and satisfied guests!

Cooking on charcoal

Before you start cooking, grease the barbecue grill with a little fat or oil to prevent the food sticking. The grill should then be positioned approximately 80 mm above the coals to seal the meat, and then raised to 100 mm.

The meat or poultry should be turned with a pair of long handled tongs or a fish slice — a fork would pierce the flesh and so release the juices.

Foil cooking is particularly useful in barbecuing — it seals in flavour and juices, and is a good way to cook small cuts of lean meat, potatoes and vegetables — mushrooms, beans and corn on the cob. Potatoes can also be parboiled first before being wrapped in foil and placed among the coals; butter and herbs added to the parcel will give extra flavour.

Preparing meat and poultry

Always choose the best quality meat for barbecuing and bring it to room temperature before placing it on the grid. If you barbecue meat that is still chilled, it will be overdone on the outside before it has a chance to cook on the inside. As a guide, big joints take about two hours to come to room temperature, steaks about one hour, and chicken pieces thirty minutes.

Trim most of the fat from the meat before cooking, otherwise it will drip into the coals, causing the fire to flare-up. Make small cuts around the remaining fat at 25 mm intervals to prevent the meat curling during cooking.

Steaks and chops should be small cuts and be about 40 mm thick. Pork should always be very thoroughly cooked. Beef steaks can be cooked in large pieces — they remain juicier this way, and can be cut up for serving.

Chicken pieces can be partially cooked in the oven first, and then placed bony side down on the grill. Alternatively, they can be placed directly on the grill (bony side down), and brushed with olive oil. When the underside is golden they can be turned until they finish cooking. The bones act as heat conductors and will speed up the cooking process — and the chicken will look good.

Whole chickens and turkeys can be cooked on a spit attachment, as can large joints of meat. Make sure that the spit is pushed through the centre of the meat, and check to see that it is well balanced so that the meat will cook evenly. Heap the charcoal at one side and insert a drip pan to catch the fat. Baste the joint with oil, butter or barbecue sauce.

Kebabs can be made up from the cheaper cuts of lamb, beef and pork and offal can also be included. Cut the meat into 25 mm pieces and thread onto skewers, alternating with vegetables such as peppers, baby onions, tomatoes and mushrooms. Baste with oil and turn frequently when cooking.

Beefburgers and sausages are always popular, especially with children. Pierce sausages before cooking to allow the fat to drain. If beefburgers are home made, place them on an oiled metal tray, as this will prevent them from falling apart.

Barbecuing fish

Fish should be cooked over a slightly higher temperature than meat or poultry. Small and large fish can be cooked whole, while large fish can also be cut into steaks or fillets. Thick fillets — such as cod — can be cubed for kebabs. To keep the fish moist, marinate fillets, steaks or kebabs and baste during cooking.

To prevent fish fillets breaking up while cooking, you can place them in a wire basket (or 'broiler'), or you can cook them on a finely meshed grid and use a metal fish slice for turning. Steaks or fillets of about 15 mm will take about 6–8 minutes to cook, turning once.

Fish can also be wrapped in a double layer of aluminium foil, which will make the cooking time longer. Dot the fish with butter and sprinkle with herbs, lemon juice, salt and black pepper before sealing well in the foil.

Unshelled cooked prawns (both small and kingsize) can be marinated then heated through for a short time on the grill.

MARINADES & BASTES

The delicious sauces you can put together for marinating (in which the meat, poultry or fish is soaked for some hours before cooking) and basting (when the food is brushed with the sauce during cooking), will add a delicious flavour to your food; marinades also help to tenderize the tougher meats. Recipes for two simple marinades, and a basting sauce, are set out below. Make sure the ingredients are covered by the marinade.

Simple Chinese marinade

4 tablespoons soy sauce
2 tablespoons red wine
1 tablespoon caster sugar
1 garlic clove, crushed

Mix together the soy sauce, red wine, caster sugar and crushed garlic until thoroughly blended. Add 2 tablespoons water and stir to dissolve the sugar.

Turkish marinade

White part of 1 leek, chopped
½ Spanish onion, chopped
6 tablespoons freshly chopped parsley
6 tablespoons olive oil
freshly ground black pepper

Combine the chopped leek, onion, parsley and oil. Add a generous amount of black pepper. Mix well.

Barbecue basting sauce

225 ml/8 fl oz tomato juice
125 ml/4 fl oz water
50 ml/2 fl oz tomato ketchup
2 tablespoons Worcester sauce
2 tablespoons light soft brown sugar
pinch of paprika
1 teaspoon mustard powder
pinch of salt
pinch of chilli powder

Mix all the ingredients in a saucepan and heat gently for 15–20 minutes, adjusting the seasoning to taste. Use to baste spareribs, sausages and burgers while grilling, and use as a sauce with plain meats.
When barbecuing allow large pieces of meat to warm up before brushing them with marinades or sauces. Brush well with a basting sauce (like the one given) for the last 15 minutes of the cooking time; this will glaze the meat without scorching.

Barbecued fruit

Pieces of apple, orange and banana can be threaded on to skewers and cooked as kebabs — having been coated with a honey glaze. Bananas are ideal — cook them in their skins for about 15 minutes and serve with a liqueur sauce.

Grilling times at a glance

Type of Food	Cut or Portion (placed 100 mm above coals)		Approximate Total Cooking Times			
			Temp of Coals*	Rare	Medium	Well-done
Beef	Burgers	15 mm	Medium-hot	8–10 min.	10–12 min.	12–15 min.
			Medium	10–12 min.	12–15 min.	15–18 min.
		25 mm	Medium-hot	10–12 min.	12–15 min.	15–18 min.
			Medium	12–15 min.	14–18 min.	18–20 min.
	Porterhouse, T-bone or sirloin steak	25 mm	Medium-hot	12–18 min.	15–20 min.	18–22 min.
		38 mm	Medium-hot	18–20 min.	20–25 min.	22–28 min.
			Medium	20–25 min.	25–30 min.	28–32 min.
Lamb	Chops	25 mm	Medium		20–25 min.	22–27 min.
		38 mm	Medium	25–30 min.	28–32 min.	30–35 min.
Pork	Chops and spareribs	25 mm	Medium			22–25 min.
		38 mm	Medium			30–35 min.
Gammon	Fully cooked slice	25 mm	Medium-hot			10–15 min.
		38 mm	Medium			25–35 min.
Chicken	Halves or quarters		Medium-hot			45–50 min.
Fish	Salmon or halibut steaks	19 mm	Medium			10–17 min.
		38 mm	Medium-hot			17–22 min.
	Trout or whitefish	approx 250 g	Medium-hot			10–17 min.
			Medium			17–20 min.

*Estimate by holding hand, palm down, about 100 mm above hot coals. Count seconds you can hold position — 2 seconds for hot coals; 3 seconds for medium-hot coals; 4 seconds for medium coals; and 5 or 6 seconds for slow coals.

MEAT & FISH DISHES

Turkey kebabs

SERVES 4

500 g/1 lb boneless turkey (breast or
 fillet) cut across the grain into
 bite-sized pieces
2 tablespoons vegetable oil
1 tablespoon lemon juice
1 tablespoon soy sauce
2 teaspoons light soft brown sugar
8 rashers streaky bacon, all rinds
 removed
1 large red pepper, deseeded and cut
 into bite-sized squares
1 small cucumber, quartered
 lengthways
freshly ground black pepper
4 thick slices white bread, crusts
 removed and cubed
vegetable oil, for greasing

PEANUT SAUCE

1 tablespoon groundnut oil
1 onion, finely chopped
½–1 teaspoon chilli powder
1 tablespoon lemon juice
2 tablespoons crunchy peanut butter
2 teaspoons soy sauce
150 ml/¼ pint coconut milk (see
 Cook's Notes)

1 Put the turkey pieces into a
shallow dish.

2 In a bowl mix together the vegetable oil, lemon juice, soy sauce and
sugar. Pour this marinade over the
turkey pieces and turn them over to
coat them. Leave in a cool place for
at least 2 hours, turning the turkey
occasionally.

3 To make the peanut sauce: heat
the oil in a frying-pan, add the onion
and fry gently for about 5 minutes
until it is soft and lightly coloured. Stir
in the chilli powder and cook for a
further 1–2 minutes. Then stir in the
lemon juice, peanut butter and soy
sauce, mixing well. Gradually stir in
the coconut milk. Pour into a bowl
and set aside.

4 Light the barbecue and when the
coals are hot grill the bacon rashers
until they are crisp. Pat dry on
absorbent paper.

5 Meanwhile, bring a small pan of
water to the boil and blanch the red
pepper for 1 minute, drain and refresh under cold water. Set aside.

6 Slice the cucumber quarters
widthways into triangle shapes and
crumble the cold bacon. Mix the
cucumber and bacon together,
season with plenty of pepper and
transfer to a suitable serving dish.

7 Remove the turkey from the

marinade with a slotted spoon and
reserve the marinade. Thread the
meat, red pepper squares and bread
cubes, in turn, on to 4 long, oiled
skewers.

8 Put the kebabs on the barbecue
grill and brush with the marinade.
Cook for 10–15 minutes turning the
kebabs and brushing them with the
marinade as you turn them. Serve at
once with the cucumber and bacon
mixture and the peanut sauce
handed separately.

COOK'S NOTES

Total preparation of the kebabs and
accompaniments takes 20–30 minutes. The meat should marinate for
at least 2 hours and the kebabs will
then take about 15 minutes to cook
through completely.

To make 150 ml/¼ pint coconut
milk, put 2 tablespoons of desiccated coconut into a jug and pour
over 150 ml/¼ pint boiling water.
Leave for 30 minutes then strain off
liquid discarding coconut.

● 450 calories/1900 kj per portion

Beef and bacon burgers

SERVES 4
225 g/8 oz streaky bacon slices
700 g/1½ lb minced beef
1 small onion
2 tablespoons chopped parsley
1 tablespoon chopped thyme
4 sage leaves, chopped
salt and freshly ground black pepper
oil for greasing
4 soft baps
salad, to garnish

1 At least 1 hour before barbecuing, heat the kitchen grill. Light the barbecue.
2 In the kitchen, grill the bacon slices on both sides until crisp. Chop them all up finely.
3 Put the minced beef into a bowl. Grate in the onion and add the herbs. Season with salt and freshly ground black pepper and mix all the ingredients together well.
4 Divide the beef mixture into 8 portions and the bacon into 4 portions. Using a hamburger press, press in one portion of the beef. Press one portion of the bacon into the beef and press another portion of beef on top. Press out into one thick burger. (This process can be done by hand if necessary.) Continue with the rest of the beef and the bacon to make 4 burgers. Put them onto a flat plate and chill for 30 minutes.
5 Place a lightly greased, flat metal plate on the barbecue grill over the hot coals. Allow it to become really hot. Put the burgers on the metal plate and cook them for 2 minutes on each side until cooked through.
6 Serve immediately in a soft bap with lettuce, tomato and cucumber or the salad of your choice.

COOK'S NOTES

Preparation of the beefburgers takes 1 hour, cooking takes only a few minutes.
Baked potatoes and salads make a good accompaniment to these tasty beefburgers which should be cooked on an oiled tray.
● 990 calories/4059 kj per portion

Dindings duck

SERVES 4

1 tablespoon ground coriander
2 teaspoons ground fenugreek
2 teaspoons ground cumin
1 teaspoon ground turmeric
1 teaspoon ground cinnamon
½ teaspoon ground cardamom
¼ teaspoon ground cloves
¼ teaspoon grated nutmeg
1 teaspoon mild chilli powder
1 teaspoon black pepper
½ teaspoon salt
½-inch piece root ginger, peeled and
  finely chopped
juice of 1 lemon
2 small onions, minced
2 garlic cloves, crushed
100 g/4 oz desiccated coconut
  soaked in 175 ml/6 fl oz boiling
  water

1 × 2.25 kg/5 lb duck, split open
through the breast bone, the ribs
broken at the backbone and the
wings and legs tied together so
that the cavity is spread open

1 Light the barbecue.
2 In a medium-sized mixing bowl,
mix all the spices together, then add
the pepper, salt, ginger, lemon juice,
onions, garlic and coconut with its
soaking liquid. Stir well to form a
thick paste. Spread the paste generously over the duck.
3 When the coals are hot, place a
drip pan under the grill and place the
duck on the grill. Cook for 2–2½
hours until tender. Baste the duck
every 15 minutes with the paste.
4 Halfway through the roasting
time, turn the duck over and baste
with the paste in the drip pan. When

the duck is cooked, baste again and
remove it from the barbecue. Pour
off the fat from the drip pan and
scrape any spice mixture from the
bottom of the pan into the cavity of
the duck.
5 Transer the duck to a warmed
serving dish and serve at once.

COOK'S NOTES

Preparation takes about 10 minutes
and cooking the duck about 2–2½
hours.
  Cooking this Malaysian dish on
the barbecue creates a wonderful
aromatic smell. Serve with cucumber and yoghurt (see page 00) or
a fresh tomato salad.
● 1182 calories/4846 kj per portion

Curried lamb chops

SERVES 4
12 thin-cut lamb chops
2 tablespoons vegetable oil
1 large onion, finely chopped
2 cloves garlic, crushed (optional)
1 tablespoon curry powder
2 teaspoons plain flour
600 ml/1 pint chicken stock
75 g/3 oz dried apricots, soaked
75 g/3 oz sultanas
4 teaspoons apricot jam
salt and freshly ground black pepper
1 teaspoon ground cumin
1 teaspoon ground cardamom
2 tablespoons desiccated coconut
coriander leaves, to garnish

1 Heat the oil in a saucepan, add the onion and garlic (if using) and cook over gentle heat for 5 minutes until soft and lightly coloured. Sprinkle in the curry powder and the flour and cook, stirring, for 1–2 minutes. Gradually add the chicken stock, stirring all the time. Bring the sauce to the boil.

2 Drain the apricots and add them with the sultanas and apricot jam to the curry sauce. Stir well and taste and adjust seasoning, if necessary. Lower the heat and simmer for 45 minutes.

3 Meanwhile light the barbecue.

4 When the coals are hot, arrange the chops on the grill. Mix together the cumin and cardamom and, using the back of a teaspoon, rub half this mixture over one side of the chops. Grill for 2–3 minutes then turn the chops over and rub in the remainder of the spice mixture. Grill for 2–3 minutes, and then grill the chops for a further 5 minutes, turning once.

5 Arrange the chops on a warmed serving dish then sprinkle with desiccated coconut and garnish with the coriander. Serve the chops at once, with the curry sauce in a warmed jug.

COOK'S NOTES

Preparing sauce takes about 5 minutes, cooking about 45 minutes. Grill the chops while the curry sauce is cooking.

Serve the chops with boiled rice, and hand round some mango chutney as well as the sauce. Two bananas, sliced and sprinkled with a little lemon juice, would also make a tasty accompaniment.

● **575 calories/2400 kj per portion**

Liver and courgette kebabs

SERVES 4

500 g/1 lb lamb's liver, cut into 2.5 cm/1 inch pieces
juice of 1 lemon
salt and freshly ground black pepper
1 teaspoon dried mixed herbs
8 streaky bacon rashers, rinds removed and cut in half crossways
4 small onions, quartered
4 small courgettes, cut into 2.5 cm/ 1 inch pieces
2 tablespoons vegetable oil, for brushing

1 Light the barbecue. Brush 4 kebab skewers with oil.
2 Brush the liver with the lemon juice and season to taste with salt and freshly ground black pepper. Sprinkle over the mixed herbs. Roll up the prepared halved bacon rashers.

3 Thread the liver, bacon rolls, quartered onions and pieces of courgette on to the kebab skewers and brush with oil.
4 When the coals are hot grill the kebabs, turning them frequently for about 4 minutes, or until cooked through.
5 When cooked, transfer the liver and courgette kebabs to a warmed serving plate and serve at once.

COOK'S NOTES

The kebabs take about 10 minutes to prepare and about 4 minutes to cook.

Serve the kebabs on a bed of boiled rice, or, for the more weight-conscious, a bed of cooked spinach.

Add some pineapple chunks, mushrooms and bacon rashers wrapped round banana slices to the kebabs.

● 390 calories/1635 kj per kebab

Stilton Steak

SERVES 4

4 rump steaks, each weighing
   175 g/6 oz (see Cook's Notes)
1 tablespoon finely chopped onion
1 tablespoon Worcestershire sauce
75 ml/3 fl oz vegetable oil
50 ml/2 fl oz port or sweet sherry
freshly ground black pepper
1 bay leaf, crumbled
75 g/3 oz Blue Stilton cheese,
   grated
watercress sprigs and tomato slices,
   to garnish

1 Put the steaks into a large shallow dish. Combine the onion, Worcestershire sauce, oil, port, pepper and bay leaf and pour over the steaks. Cover and leave to marinate for at least 3 hours at room temperature, turning the steaks several times.

2 Meanwhile, light the barbecue.

3 When the coals are hot, using a fish slice, lift the steaks from the marinade and arrange them on the grill rack. Grill for about 5 minutes, depending on whether you like your steak rare or medium, basting from time to time with the marinade. Turn the steaks and grill for 2–5 minutes.

4 Sprinkle the Stilton over each steak, dividing it equally between them and pressing down with the back of a spoon. Grill for a further 3 minutes until the Stilton topping is melted and bubbling.

5 Transfer the steaks to a warmed serving dish, garnish with watercress and tomato and serve at once.

COOK'S NOTES

Allow at least 3 hours marinating time. Cooking takes about 10 minutes.

Rump steak is cut from the lower part of the sirloin. Choose rump steaks that have a slightly purplish tinge which shows that they have been well-hung and will be tender. Some supermarkets sell smallish pieces of rump steak in special economy packs: these would be ideal.

Frying steak, which is much cheaper than rump steak, may be used instead; it will need to be cooked for slightly longer.

If steaks are marinated there is no need to beat the meat to tenderize it. The alcohol in the marinade will break down fibres of the meat.

Serve the steaks with baked potatoes and a green salad.

● 380 calories/1600 kj per portion

Soya chicken with mustard sauce

SERVES 4

8 chicken thighs, each weighing about 150 g/5 oz
spring onion tassels, to garnish (optional)

MARINADE

125 ml/4 fl oz soy sauce
1 tablespoon vegetable oil
2 tablespoons light soft brown sugar
2 tablespoons brandy or whisky
1 clove garlic, crushed (optional)
freshly ground black pepper

SAUCE

4 tablespoons thick bottled mayonnaise
4 tablespoons natural yoghurt
1 tablespoon mustard powder
2 spring onions, finely chopped

1 Mix all the marinade ingredients together. Place the chicken in a bowl and spoon over the marinade. Set aside in a cool place for 8 hours, or overnight, turning occasionally.
2 Light the barbecue.
3 When the coals are hot place the chicken thighs on the grill and baste with marinade. Cook for 15–20 minutes, turning and basting frequently until the juices run clear when the thickest part of the meat is pierced with a skewer.
4 Meanwhile, make the sauce: mix all the ingredients together, then transfer to a serving bowl and refrigerate until required.
5 To serve, transfer the chicken to a warmed serving dish and spoon over the remaining liquid from the drip pan. Serve at once, garnished with the spring onion tassels, if using. Hand the sauce separately.

COOK'S NOTES

Preparation takes about 10 minutes, cooking 15–20 minutes, but allow at least 8 hours or soaking overnight for the chicken to marinate.

This marinade also goes well with pork.

The chicken can also be served cold, if liked.

Serve with stir-fried beansprouts, or with a beansprout and endive salad.

Sherry can be used in place of the brandy or whisky but will not give such a strong flavour.

● **760 calories/3175 kj per portion**

Kid's kebabs

SERVES 4

175 g/6 oz unsliced wholemeal bread, crust removed
250 g/9 oz Edam or Gruyère cheese (see Cook's Notes)
1 thick slice cooked ham, weighing about 40 g/1½ oz (see Cook's Notes)
25 g/1 oz butter, melted
vegetable oil, for greasing

1 Light the barbecue and oil 4 kebab skewers.
2 Cut the bread and cheese into 2.5 cm/1 inch cubes and the ham into 2.5 cm/1 inch squares.
3 Arrange the pieces of bread, cheese and ham on the skewers, alternating the ingredients. Brush kebabs with melted butter.
4 When the coals are hot, grill the kebabs, turning several times, for about 5 minutes or until the bread is brown and the cheese is beginning to melt. Serve at once, either on or off the skewers (see Cook's Notes).

COOK'S NOTES

Preparation takes 10 minutes and the cooking time is about 5 minutes.

Children will enjoy assembling these kebabs which make a quick and easy barbecue meal for them. Serve with baked beans or grilled tomatoes. Scrambled eggs can also be served with the kebabs, to make a more substantial meal.

Try spreading the bread with peanut butter or Marmite before threading it on the skewers. Spread mustard on the bread for grown-ps' kebabs. A combination of red Leicester and mature Cheddar cheeses gives the kebabs a colourful appearance. Squares of salami or luncheon meat may be used instead of ham.

● **315 calories/1300 kj per portion**

Scallop and bacon kebabs

SERVES 4

500 g/1 lb frozen scallops, defrosted and halved (see Cook's Notes)
150 ml/¼ pint fish stock (see Cook's Notes)
salt and freshly ground black pepper
3 tablespoons finely chopped fresh parsley
1 clove garlic, finely chopped (optional)
10 slices streaky bacon, rinds removed, stretched with the back of a knife and halved
40 g/1½ oz butter, melted
4 lemon wedges, to garnish

1 Light the barbecue. Brush 4 kebab skewers with oil.
2 Put the scallops into a saucepan and pour over the fish stock. Season with salt and pepper.
3 Bring to the boil over moderate heat, then lower the heat, cover the pan and simmer for 5 minutes. Drain the scallops well and pat them dry with absorbent paper.
4 Spread out the parsley and garlic, if using, on a flat plate. Roll the scallops in the parsley until evenly covered. Set aside.
5 Roll up pieces of bacon neatly. Thread the pieces of scallop and the streaky bacon rolls alternately on to the metal kebab skewers.
6 When the coals are hot place the kebabs on the grill rack and brush with melted butter. Cook for about 10–12 minutes, turning and basting kebabs frequently.
7 Arrange the cooked kebabs on a warmed serving plate. Garnish with some lemon wedges and serve at once, while they are still very hot (see Cook's Notes).

COOK'S NOTES

Preparation takes about 20 minutes and cooking the kebabs 10–12 minutes.

Use large frozen scallops which can be cut in half to give enough pieces. Some scallops may have the pink roe, coral as it is called, still attached. This can be left on.

Fish stock cubes are available from some delicatessens. If they are difficult to obtain, use homemade chicken stock or ¼ chicken stock cube.

Serve the scallop and bacon kebabs with a tasty mixed salad or, alternatively, serve them up on a bed of boiled rice.

● 250 calories/1050 kj per portion

Tandoori fish

SERVES 4

750 g–1 kg/1½–2 lb haddock
    fillets, skinned and cut into
    4 pieces
lemon wedges, to garnish

MARINADE

150 g/5 oz natural yoghurt
juice of 1 lemon
1 onion, grated
1 teaspoon ground cumin
2 teaspoons sweet paprika
good pinch of cayenne pepper
salt

1 Rinse the fish and pat dry with absorbent paper.
2 To make the marinade: in a small bowl, mix the yoghurt with the lemon juice, grated onion, cumin, sweet paprika, cayenne and 1 teaspoon salt.
3 Sprinkle the fish on both sides with salt, place on a large plate and spread with half the yoghurt mixture, then turn the pieces over and spread with the remaining mixture. Cover the plate and leave the fish to marinate in a cool place for at least 1 hour.
4 Meanwhile, light the barbecue. When the coals are hot, remove the fish from the marinade and place on the grill in a hinged wire basket,

skinned side up. Reserve any yoghurt mixture left on the plate. Grill the fish for 5 minutes on one side, then carefully turn the pieces over and spread with the reserved yoghurt mixture and grill for about a further 5–7 minutes until the fish is cooked through and the topping is a golden brown.
5 Transfer the fish to a warmed serving platter, garnish with lemon wedges and serve at once.

COOK'S NOTES

15 minutes preparation, at least 1 hour marinating, then 10–12 minutes cooking.

    Serve the tasty tandoori fish with boiled rice and a fresh, light cucumber salad.

● 185 calories/775 kj per portion

Saucy fish skewers

SERVES 4

750 g/1½ lb cod fillet, skinned and
  cut into 2.5 cm/1 inch cubes
  (see Cook's Notes)
1 green pepper, deseeded and cut
  into 2 cm/¾ inch dice
4 small tomatoes, halved
8 small button mushrooms
vegetable oil, for greasing

MARINADE

juice of 2 lemons
2 thinly pared strips of lemon zest,
  about 5 cm/2 inches long
  150 ml/¼ pint olive oil
3 tablespoons chopped fresh parsley
1 clove garlic, crushed
salt and freshly ground black pepper

SAUCE

2 tablespoons plain flour
300 ml/½ pint milk
1 tablespoon chopped fresh parsley

1 Put all the marinade ingredients
into a glass or china bowl with salt
and pepper to taste. Add the fish
cubes and turn carefully in the marinade to coat thoroughly. Cover and
refrigerate for at least 6 hours, stirring
occasionally.
2 Light the barbecue, and oil some
kebab skewers (use barbecue
skewers for ease).
3 Remove the fish cubes from the
marinade, carefully shaking off any
excess. Reserve the marinade.
4 Thread the fish cubes onto the
oiled kebab skewers, alternating each
fish cube with a piece of green pepper, a tomato half or a mushroom.
5 When the coals are hot, place the
kebabs on the grill, brush with a little
of the reserved marinade and grill for
about 10 minutes, turning once or
twice, until the fish is cooked through
and golden.
6 Meanwhile, make the sauce: pour
the remaining marinade into a small
saucepan, discarding the lemon zest.
Set over a low heat, sprinkle in the
flour and cook, stirring, for 1–2
minutes. Remove from the heat and
gradually stir in the milk.
7 Return to the heat and simmer,

stirring, until thick and smooth. Stir
in the parsley and season with salt
and pepper.
8 Transfer the cooked kebabs to a
warmed serving platter and spoon
over a little of the sauce. Hand the
remaining sauce separately in a
warmed sauceboat.

COOK'S NOTES

Preparation takes 10 minutes. Allow
at least 6 hours for marinating,
cooking then takes 10 minutes.
  Serve the kebabs on a bed of
nutty, brown rice and accompany
them with French or runner beans.
  Turn the fish carefully in the
marinade so that the fish does not
break up.
  Use other less expensive firm
white fish such as coley, huss or
rock salmon.
● 520 calories/2175 kj per portion

Wholemeal stuffed trout

SERVES 4

4 trout, scaled and cleaned, each
  weighing 250–300 g/9–11 oz
75 g/3 oz margarine or butter
75 g/3 oz streaky bacon rashers,
  rinds removed and finely chopped
1 small onion, finely chopped
75 g/3 oz wholemeal breadcrumbs
grated zest and juice of ½ lemon
1½ tablespoons chopped fresh
  parsley
1½ teaspoons dried thyme
1½ teaspoons dried marjoram
salt and freshly ground black pepper
25 g/1 oz wholemeal flour

1 Light the barbecue.
2 Wash the trout inside and out and remove any loose scales and all the blood from alongside the backbone. Pat the fish dry with absorbent paper.
3 Melt 25 g/1 oz of the margarine in a frying-pan, add the bacon and onion and fry over moderate heat for 5 minutes until the onion is soft and lightly coloured.
4 Remove the pan from the heat and stir in the breadcrumbs, lemon juice and about two-thirds of the herbs. Season with salt and pepper to taste.
5 Divide the stuffing into 4 portions and stuff each fish. Reshape fish.
6 On a large flat plate, mix together the flour, lemon zest and remaining herbs. Add salt and pepper to taste. Roll the trout gently in the mixture to coat evenly.
7 Lay the trout in a hinged wire basket on the hot barbecue grill and dot them with half the margarine. Grill them for 4–5 minutes, then turn them over with a fish slice, dot with the remaining margarine and grill for about a further 4–5 minutes until cooked through and browned. Transfer to a warmed serving platter and serve at once.

COOK'S NOTES

Preparation and cooking will take about 1 hour.

Use herring instead of trout, and the dish will be less expensive. You may leave out the bacon and the main flavour in the stuffing will come from the herbs.

If fresh herbs are available, use 1 tablespoon each fresh thyme and marjoram. Lemon thyme, with its definite scent and taste of lemon, goes particularly well with fish.

● 540 calories/2250 kj per portion

Turkish lamb kebabs

SERVES 6

1 kg/2 lb boneless lamb, trimmed of
   excess fat and cut into 2.5 cm/
   1 inch cubes (see Cook's Notes)
1 large green pepper, deseeded and
   cut into 2.5 cm/1 inch cubes
1 large tomato, cut into chunks
6 button onions (see Cook's Notes)
2 courgettes, thickly sliced
1 lemon, cut into chunks
vegetable oil, for greasing

MARINADE

6 tablespoons olive oil
4 tablespoons dry sherry
1 clove garlic, crushed
½ onion, finely chopped
2 tablespoons finely chopped fresh
   parsley
1 teaspoon dried oregano
freshly ground black pepper

1 Make the marinade: put the olive oil in a large bowl. Add the sherry, garlic, onion, parsley, oregano and a generous sprinkling of freshly ground black pepper. Mix well.

2 Add the lamb cubes to the marinade, turn to coat well, then cover and refrigerate for at least 8 hours, turning the meat several times.

3 Light the barbecue and oil 6 skewers.

4 Drain the meat, reserving the marinade. Thread the meat on to the oiled skewers, alternating with the green pepper squares, tomato chunks, button onions, courgette slices and lemon chunks.

5 When the coals are hot, brush the grill with oil and brush the kebabs with the reserved marinade. Place the kebabs on the grill and cook for 10–15 minutes, turning frequently and basting with the remaining marinade.

6 Transfer the kebabs to a warmed serving plate and serve at once.

COOK'S NOTES

Preparation 30 minutes, but allow at least 8 hours for marinating. Cooking takes 10–15 minutes.

Buy best lean lamb, preferably cut from the fillet or top end of leg.

If you prefer onions to be well cooked, poach the button onions in water for 5 minutes before threading on to the skewers.

The kebabs are delicious served with pitta bread that has been heated through on the barbecue. Offer finely shredded lettuce and cucumber and tomato slices to pack into the pitta bread with the meat.

For an attractive finish, garnish the kebabs with lemon wedges or lemon twists dipped in finely chopped fresh parsley.

● 440 calories/1850 kj per portion

Barbecued chicken with lemon

SERVES 4
1.5 kg/3–3½ lb oven-ready chicken,
   thoroughly defrosted if frozen,
   divided into quarters
vegetable oil, for greasing
8 lemon wedges, to garnish

MARINADE
75 ml/3 fl oz olive oil
3 tablespoons lemon juice
½ small onion, finely chopped
2 teaspoons chopped fresh tarragon
   or 1 teaspoon dried tarragon
salt and freshly ground black pepper

1 Make the marinade: put the olive oil in a shallow bowl together with the lemon juice, chopped onion, tarragon and salt and pepper to taste. Mix well, then add the chicken pieces and turn to coat well. Leave to marinate for 8 hours or overnight in the refrigerator.
2 Light the barbecue.
3 Remove the marinated chicken from the refrigerator and leave to stand at room temperature.
4 When the coals are hot, brush the grill with oil, lift the chicken pieces from the marinade and place on the grill. Reserve the marinade.
5 Cook the chicken pieces for about 40 minutes until cooked through (see Cook's Notes), turning and brushing the chicken with the reserved marinade.
6 Transfer the chicken to a warmed serving plate, garnish with lemon wedges and serve at once.

COOK'S NOTES

Preparation takes 15 minutes, plus at least 8 hours marinating time. Cooking takes about 40 minutes.

To test if the chicken is done, pierce the thickest part of the flesh with a skewer — the juices will run clear if it is cooked through.

Fresh tarragon strips, when available, make an attractive additional garnish to the chicken.

Serve with plain boiled rice — for extra colour, stir 1 tablespoon finely chopped fresh parsley into the rice. Lightly cooked green beans make an excellent vegetable accompaniment.

To spice up the marinade, try adding a few drops of Tabasco sauce to the mixture.

● 565 calories/2375 kj per portion

Barbecued spareribs

SERVES 6

1.5 kg /3–3½ lb pork spareribs,
  Chinese style (see Cook's Notes)
vegetable oil, for greasing

MARINADE

75 ml/3 fl oz soy sauce
300 ml/½ pint tomato ketchup
150 ml/¼ pint dry white wine
50 g/2 oz soft brown sugar
1 large clove garlic, finely chopped
pinch of ground coriander
pinch of chilli powder
pinch of ground cinnamon
½ teaspoon mixed dried herbs
salt and freshly ground black pepper

1 Make the marinade: put the soy sauce in a large shallow bowl together with the tomato ketchup, dry white wine and brown sugar. Stir until the sugar has dissolved, then add the garlic, spices, herbs and salt and pepper to taste. Stir to mix well.

2 Add the spareribs to the marinade and turn until well coated. Leave to marinate for 8 hours or overnight in the refrigerator. The marinade should thoroughly coat the ribs; if necessary, make up some more in the same quantities as given above.

3 Light the barbecue.

4 Remove the bowl of spareribs from the refrigerator and leave to stand at room temperature.

5 When the coals are hot, brush the grill with oil, then lift the spareribs from the dish and place on the grill. Allow any excess marinade to drip off the ribs.

6 Cook for 20 minutes, turning constantly and brushing with the marinade.

7 Move the spareribs to the cooler edge of the grill and cook for a further 5–10 minutes until cooked through. Serve at once.

COOK'S NOTES

Preparation takes about 15 minutes, cooking 25–30 minutes, but allow at least 8 hours or soak overnight for the spareribs to marinate.

Buy sheets of Chinese-style spareribs for this recipe, not sparerib chops. These are available ready cut from some large supermarkets; most family butchers also sell them.

For a colourful meal, serve the spareribs with strips of crunchy raw vegetables, such as carrots, cucumber and red pepper, accompanied by a tangy dip. For the dip mix soured cream with a touch of horseradish sauce, snipped chives and crushed garlic.

● 355 calories/1475 kj per portion

Gammon steaks in foil

SERVES 4

**4 gammon steaks, about 1 cm/
  ½ inch thick
50 g/2 oz butter
2 tablespoons olive oil
1 large onion, thinly sliced
8 button mushrooms, thinly sliced
1 tablespoon lemon juice
2 tablespoons finely chopped fresh
  parsley
4 tablespoons tomato purée
150 ml/¼ pint dry white wine
sprigs of watercress, to garnish**

1 Heat the butter and oil in a small saucepan, add the sliced onions and fry gently for 5 minutes until soft and lightly coloured. Add the mushrooms and cook gently for 2 minutes, or until soft.

2 Sprinkle the lemon juice and chopped parsley into the pan, then remove the pan from the heat. Stir in the tomato purée and dry white wine and leave to cool.

3 Light the barbecue.

4 Cut 4 squares of foil large enough to enclose the gammon steaks. Spread one eighth of the vegetable mixture in the centre of each square of foil, then place a gammon steak on top of each square. Spread the remaining vegetable mixture over the gammon steaks, then seal the foil to form neat parcels.

5 When the coals are hot, arrange the parcels on the grill, join upwards, and cook for 12–16 minutes until thoroughly cooked through.

6 To serve: open the foil wrappings and garnish the gammon steaks with sprigs of watercress.

COOK'S NOTES

Preparation takes 20 minutes, but allow time for the vegetable mixture to cool. Cooking takes 12–16 minutes in total.

For an extravagant touch, reduce the amount of wine to 6 tablespoons and add 2 tablespoons of brandy at the end of stage 2.

Serve with new potatoes tossed in butter and sprinkled with chopped fresh parsley. A mixed green salad would also make a good accompaniment.

● **605 calories/2525 kj per portion**

Skewered kidneys

SERVES 4

**12 lamb's kidneys, skinned and
  halved, with cores removed**
4 tablespoons melted butter
100 g/4 oz fresh white breadcrumbs
4 back bacon rashers
**vegetable oil, for brushing and
  greasing**
sprigs of watercress to garnish

GARLIC BUTTER

100 g/4 oz butter, softened
2 cloves garlic, crushed
**1 tablespoon finely chopped fresh
  parsley**
salt and freshly ground black pepper

1 Make the garlic butter: in a small bowl, beat the softened butter with the garlic, parsley and salt and pepper to taste. Spoon the butter on to a piece of greaseproof paper, fold the paper over and shape the butter into a neat roll, about 2.5 cm/1 inch wide. Pat the ends of the roll to flatten and neaten, then twist the ends of the greaseproof paper. Chill in the refrigerator for about 1 hour or until firm.

2 Light the barbecue and oil 5 skewers.

3 Spread the breadcrumbs out on a plate. Brush the kidneys with the melted butter, then toss in the breadcrumbs to coat evenly. Shake off any excess breadcrumbs and thread the kidneys on to 4 oiled skewers.

4 Cut each bacon rasher into 3 lengthways, then roll up each piece and thread all the rolls on to one oiled skewer.

5 When the coals are hot, brush the grill with oil. Place the kidney skewers on the grill and cook for 8–10 minutes until the kidneys are tender but still slightly pink in the middle. Turn and brush with oil from time to time to ensure that they keep moist.

6 Meanwhile, place the bacon skewer on the grill and cook for 4–6 minutes until golden, turning fre-quently. Remove the bacon rolls from the skewer.

7 Arrange the cooked kidney skewers on a warmed serving plate. Cut the garlic butter into slices and arrange on top of the kidneys. Scatter the bacon rolls over the top and garnish with watercress sprigs. Serve at once.

COOK'S NOTES

Preparation takes about 40 minutes, plus chilling the butter. Cooking is about 10 minutes.

The garlic butter is perfect for garnishing other barbecued food — it is particularly good with steaks.

If you prefer, the garlic may be omitted from the butter and the amount of parsley increased to 3 tablespoons.

For a complete meal, serve the kidneys with noodles tossed in butter, plus lightly fried courgettes.
● **595 calories/2475 kj per portion**

Veal roll kebabs

SERVES 4

8 thin veal escalopes, each weighing
   75 g/3 oz (see Cook's Notes)
freshly ground black pepper
olive oil, for brushing and greasing
8 button onions
1 large red pepper, deseeded and cut
   into eight pieces
1 large green pepper, deseeded and
   cut into eight pieces
8 small tomatoes

FILLING
25 g/1 oz butter
100 g/4 oz streaky bacon rashers,
   rinds removed and finely chopped
2 cloves garlic, crushed
1 tablespoon finely chopped fresh
   parsley
salt

1 Season the escalopes with a generous sprinkling of pepper.
2 Make the filling: melt the butter in
a small frying-pan. Add the bacon
and garlic and fry over moderate
heat for 5 minutes until lightly
browned. Stir in the parsley and
season to taste with salt and pepper.
Remove from heat and leave to cool.
3 Divide the filling among the
8 escalopes, then tightly roll up each
escalope around the filling. Tie each
roll in 2 places with fine string, then
brush with olive oil and leave for
10 minutes to allow the flavours to
mingle.
4 Light the barbecue and oil
8 skewers.
5 Assemble the kebabs: first thread
on a button onion, then a piece of
red pepper, a prepared veal roll
(lengthways), a piece of green
pepper and finally a small tomato.
6 When the coals are hot, brush
the grill with oil. Cook the kebabs
for 10–12 minutes until the veal
is cooked and the peppers are
blistered. Turn frequently during
cooking and brush occasionally with
olive oil.
7 Transfer the kebabs to a warmed
serving plate, remove the strings
from the veal rolls and serve at once.

COOK'S NOTES

Preparation takes about 1 hour,
cooking 10–12 minutes.

To beat the escalopes flat, place
them between 2 sheets of greaseproof paper and beat them with a
wooden mallet or rolling pin to a
thickness of 5 mm/¼ inch.

Pork tenderloin makes a good and
less expensive alternative to veal.
Turkey escalopes can also be used.

Serve with vegetables cooked in
foil parcels on the grill of the barbecue — try sweetcorn wrapped with
a knob of butter and a sprinkling of
black pepper, or thinly sliced mushrooms with a sprinkling of lemon
juice and finely chopped fresh herbs.
Hot herbed bread would also make a
good accompaniment.
● 335 calories/1400 kj per portion

TEMPTING APPETIZERS

Garlic bread

MAKES 16–20 PORTIONS
225 g/8 oz butter, softened
2 tablespoons finely chopped fresh parsley
2 garlic cloves, very finely chopped
2 long loaves of French bread

1 In a small mixing bowl, cream the butter, parsley and garlic together with a wooden spoon. With a large knife, thickly slice the loaves cross-ways to within about 1 cm/¼ inch of the bottom.

2 Spread the butter mixture generously on one side of each of the slices. Wrap the loaves in aluminium foil and place them on a baking sheet in the centre of the oven. Bake for 15 to 20 minutes, or until the bread is very crusty and the butter has melted.

4 Remove the loaves from the oven and serve immediately, in the foil.

COOK'S NOTES

Garlic bread is always a popular appetizer with party guests.

You can also warm up garlic bread on the barbecue. Wrap in heavy-duty aluminium foil, dull side out, and barbecue on the grill about 10–13 cm (4–5 in) above the coals. Heat for about 10 minutes turning several times. Open the foil in the last few minutes to allow the char-coal flavour to permeate the bread.

● 565 calories/2375 kj per portion

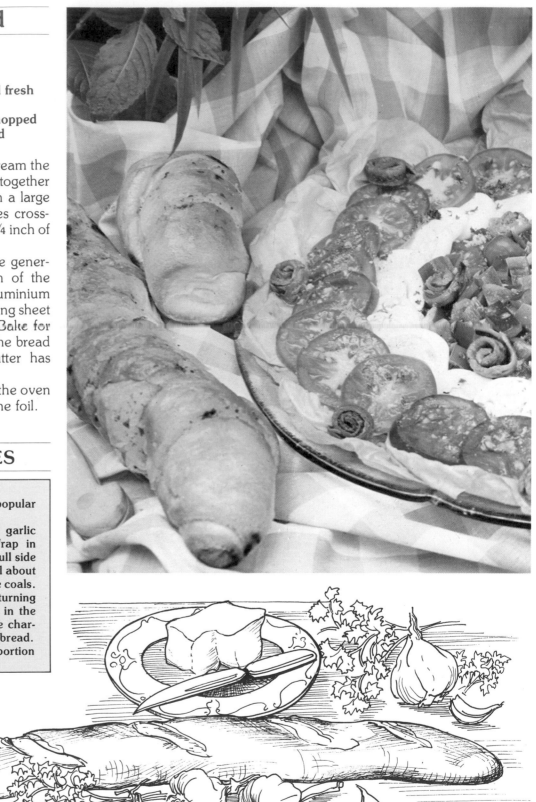

Peanut and chicken savouries

SERVES 4

250 g/9 oz cooked chicken, minced or finely chopped
3 tablespoons crunchy peanut butter
1 tablespoon chopped fresh parsley
1 teaspoon grated onion
25 g/1 oz margarine or butter, softened
1 tablespoon milk
salt and freshly ground black pepper
1 small French loaf
2 tomatoes, sliced

1 Heat the grill to moderate.
2 Put the chicken, peanut butter, parsley, onion, margarine and milk into a bowl. Season to taste with salt and pepper, then mix until all the ingredients are thoroughly blended.
3 Cut the bread into 2.5 cm/1 inch slices, discarding the ends. Toast on one side then remove from the grill, and spread the untoasted sides with the chicken mixture. Top each slice with a slice of tomato.
4 Return to the grill for 3–4 minutes until golden. Serve at once.

COOK'S NOTES

Preparation takes 15 minutes; cooking time is only 6–8 minutes.

This is an ideal way of using left-over roast chicken while at the same time providing a filling snack.

The mixture quickly browns, so make sure the grill is not too high and the cooked time is followed.

These savouries make tempting appetizers for a summer barbecue party.

● 435 calories/1835 kj per portion

Savoury stuffed tomatoes

SERVES 4

3 tablespoons olive oil (see Cook's Notes)
100 g/4 oz smoked streaky bacon, rinds removed and chopped
100 g/4 oz mushrooms, thinly sliced (see Cook's Notes)
2 onions thinly sliced
4 large or 8 medium tomatoes, total weight about 750 g/1½ lb
1 egg, beaten
salt and freshly ground black pepper
50 g/2 oz fresh white breadcrumbs

1 Heat the oven to 180C/350F/Gas 4.

2 Heat 2 tablespoons of the olive oil in a frying-pan, add the bacon, mushrooms and onions and stir well. Cook over gentle heat for 10–12 minutes, until the mixture is soft but not brown. Remove from the heat.

3 Meanwhile, cut the tomatoes in half crossways and then scoop out all the seeds with a teaspoon, taking care not to pierce the shells. Arrange the tomatoes in a single layer in an ovenproof dish.

4 Stir the egg into the bacon, mushroom and onion mixture. Mix well and season with salt and pepper. Spoon the mixture into the prepared tomato shells, packing it in well.

5 Sprinkle the stuffed tomatoes with the remaining olive oil and top with the breadcrumbs, pressing them down with the back of a teaspoon. Cook in the oven, just below centre, for 35 minutes. Raise the oven heat to 200C/400F/Gas 6 and cook for a further 10 minutes. Serve at once.

COOK'S NOTES

Preparation takes 30 minutes; cooking in the oven, 45 minutes.

If you have to use smaller tomatoes, do not halve them but slice off a lid before scooping out the flesh.

If liked, add 1 tablespoon finely chopped parsley or a pinch of dried basil to the stuffing mixture before cooking the tomatoes.

Serve these tasty tomatoes with barbecued chicken fish.

Use large open mushrooms rather than the button type for a more pronounced 'mushroomy' flavour.

Use vegetable oil, instead of olive oil, but the flavour will not be as good.

● 290 calories/1225 kj per portion

Chilled cucumber soup

SERVES 4

1 large cucumber, finely grated
   (see Cook's Notes)
450 g/16 oz natural yoghurt
2 tablespoons wine vinegar
2 tablespoons chopped fresh dill, or
   2 teaspoons dried dillweed
2 tablespoons seedless raisins
2 hard-boiled eggs, finely chopped
1 large clove garlic, crushed
(optional)
1 teaspoon caster sugar
1 large crisp dessert apple, cored
   and chopped
150 ml/¼ pint soured cream

1   In a large bowl combine all the ingredients and stir well to mix them
thoroughly.
2   Cover the bowl and refrigerate for
at least 3 hours (see Cook's Notes).
3   Pour the soup into a tureen or
spoon straight into individual bowls
and serve very cold.

COOK'S NOTES

Total preparation time is 40 minutes. Allow at least 3 hours for chilling.

Do not remove the cucumber peel unless it is very tough.

If you are short of time, chill the soup in the freezer or refrigerator freezing compartment for 30 minutes.

Try mint or tarragon instead of dill. Crisp vegetables such as celery, fennel and radishes may be used instead of the apple.

This is a Persian version of an uncooked soup that is enormously popular throughout the Middle East. Cucumber and yoghurt is a favourite combination in Middle Eastern countries because its refreshing qualities are particularly suited to the hot climate.

Reserve a little cucumber, slice it very thinly and float it on top of the soup with a sprig of dill, mint or tarragon, according to which herb is used in the recipe. This is a perfect soup to start off a barbecue party.

● 230 calories/950 kj per portion

Cucumber and yoghurt salad

SERVES 4

1 large cucumber, coarsely grated
  (see Cook's Notes)
1 teaspoon salt
2 × 150 g/5 oz cartons natural
  yoghurt
1 large clove garlic, crushed
1–2 tablespoons chopped mint
freshly ground black pepper
fresh mint sprigs, to garnish
hot pitta bread, to serve

1 Put the grated cucumber into a large bowl, sprinkle with the salt and leave to stand for 30 minutes.
2 Turn the salted cucumber into a colander and then rinse under cold running water. Drain cucumber and return to rinsed-out bowl.
3 Stir in the yoghurt, together with the garlic, mint and pepper to taste.
4 Alternatively, for a smoother mixture, purée the yoghurt and cucumber in a blender or food processor.
5 Cover the salad and refrigerate for 2–3 hours until well chilled.
6 Serve the salad in a bowl on a large serving plate. Garnish with mint and serve at once with hot pitta bread (see Cook's Notes) or with a selection of raw vegetables such as carrot, celery and peppers cut into matchstick strips.

COOK'S NOTES

This refreshing salad takes about 45 minutes to make, including salting time. Allow 2–3 hours chilling.

This salad originated in Turkey, where it is known as *cacik*, but different versions are found in the countries stretching from the Near East to India.

In Greece this salad is called *tsatsiki*, while in India, where it is flavoured with cumin and cayenne, it is known as *khira raita*. A Middle Eastern custom is to sprinkle the top with paprika and pour over 1–2 tablespoons olive oil before serving.

It is not necessary to peel the cucumber, unless the skin is very tough.

● 50 calories/200 kj per portion.

Cucumber scoops with dip

SERVES 4
1 large cucumber
1 teaspoon chopped fresh dill
salt and freshly ground black pepper
dill sprig, to garnish (optional)

DIP
500 g/1 lb carton natural yoghurt, chilled (see Cook's Notes)
100 g/4 oz walnut pieces, roughly chopped
1 clove garlic, crushed (optional)
1 teaspoon sweet paprika
¼–½ teaspoon chilli powder

1 Cut the cucumber into 5 cm/ 2 inch chunks. Cut each cucumber chunk into quarters, lengthways, then sprinkle with the chopped dill and salt and black pepper to taste.
2 Make the dip: put the yoghurt into a bowl and stir lightly with a fork. Add the walnuts, garlic (if using), paprika and chilli. Season generously with salt and pepper. Mix with the fork until well blended, then transfer to a small serving bowl.
3 Put the bowl of dip in the centre of a large serving plate, garnish with a dill sprig and arrange the cucumber around the edge.

COOK'S NOTES

This unusual idea for a light dip takes only 15 minutes to prepare.

This dip should be served at once; if left for more than 30 minutes the walnuts lose their crispness and may become a little bitter.

If possible, try to buy thick or 'firm set' yoghurt, so that the dip has enough body to be scooped up on to the cucumber wedges. If only thin yoghurt is available, replace a little of it with curd or cottage cheese to add thickness.

Refreshing cucumber wedges with a yoghurt-based dip makes a perfect summery first course. This dish is also delicious served as a side salad with curries and other spicy dishes.

● 210 calories/875 kj per portion

Cheese-stuffed courgettes

SERVES 4

4 large courgettes
salt
1 tablespoon vegetable oil
1 onion, chopped
225 g/8 oz cottage cheese, sieved
50 g/2 oz Parmesan cheese, grated
1 egg, beaten
1 tablespoon finely chopped parsley
freshly ground black pepper
4 tablespoons day-old soft white
**   breadcrumbs**
50 g/2 oz Cheddar cheese, grated
50 g/2 oz margarine or butter,
**   melted**
margarine, for greasing

1 Heat the oven to 200C/400F/ Gas 6.
2 Bring a large saucepan of salted water to the boil, add the courgettes, bring back to the boil, reduce the heat and simmer for about 10 minutes until barely tender. Drain and refresh under cold running water for 1 minute. Drain thoroughly again.
3 Cut the courgettes into half lengthways and with a teaspoon or grapefruit knife carefully scrape out the core and seeds from the centre, leaving a good shell. Reserve the scooped-out flesh and seeds (see Cook's Notes). Sprinkle the insides of the courgettes with salt, place upside down on absorbent paper and leave to drain for 5–10 minutes.
4 Meanwhile, chop the reserved courgette flesh. Heat the oil in a frying-pan, add the onion and courgette flesh and fry over moderate heat for about 10 minutes until the onion is just beginning to brown. Transfer to a bowl and leave to cool.
5 Mix the cottage cheese with the onion and courgette mixture. Stir in the Parmesan cheese, egg and parsley and season to taste with salt and pepper. The mixture should hold its shape: if it is too soft, add a few of the breadcrumbs.
6 Grease a large shallow ovenproof dish and place the courgette halves in it in a single layer, skin side down. Using a teaspoon, fill the courgettes with the stuffing, heaping it in a mound on each half.
7 Mix together the breadcrumbs and grated Cheddar cheese and sprinkle evenly over the courgettes. Drizzle the melted margarine or butter over the top and bake in the oven for 25–30 minutes until golden and bubbling. Serve hot.

COOK'S NOTES

Preparation and cooking take 55 minutes.
    Do not overcook the courgettes at this stage: they should still be firm or they will disintegrate when baked.
    Serve as a tasty appetizer on a summer evening.
    There is no need to discard the courgette seeds: when mixed and cooked with the other stuffing ingredients they will not be noticeable.
● **330 calories/1375 kj per portion**

Prawn puffs

MAKES 8

100 g/4 oz peeled prawns, chopped
1 tablespoon margarine or butter
1 small onion, finely chopped
½ small red or green pepper,
  deseeded and finely chopped
75 g/3 oz full-fat soft cheese
1 tablespoon soured cream
1 teaspoon lemon juice
2–3 teaspoons horseradish relish
2 teaspoons fine white breadcrumbs
salt and freshly ground black pepper
215 g/7½ oz frozen puff pastry,
  defrosted
1 egg, beaten, to seal and glaze

1 Melt the margarine in a frying-pan. Add the onion and fry gently for 3–4 minutes until soft but not coloured. Add the red or green pepper and cook for a further 3 minutes until softened. Remove from the heat and stir in the prawns, cheese, soured cream, lemon juice, horseradish relish and breadcrumbs, then season to taste with salt and pepper.

Set aside to cool for about 30 minutes.

2 Heat the oven to 220C/425F/Gas 7. Dampen a baking sheet with cold water.

3 Roll out the pastry on a lightly floured surface. Trim it to a rectangle 40 × 20 cm/16 × 8 inches, then use a sharp knife to cut it into eight 10 cm/4 inch squares. Divide the prawn mixture between the squares, leaving a 1 cm/½ inch border. Brush the edges of the pastry with beaten egg then fold each square into a triangle. Press the edges firmly together to seal them, then knock up with the back of a knife. Brush the tops with beaten egg, then use a sharp knife to make 2 slits to allow steam to escape.

4 Using a fish slice, carefully transfer the triangles to the prepared sheet. Bake in the oven for 10–15 minutes, or until well risen and golden brown. Serve hot or cold.

COOK'S NOTES

Preparation takes 25 minutes, cooking 10–15 minutes, but allow another 30 minutes for the prawn mixture to cool.

Serve the puffs at the beginning of a summer buffet party.

Use ham or tongue instead of prawns, and replace the red or green pepper with 50 g/2 oz sliced mushrooms.

● 185 calories/775 kj per puff

71

Sesame chicken fingers

SERVES 4

4 boneless chicken breasts (each weighing about 275 g/10 oz), skinned (see Cook's Notes)
75 g/3 oz fine stale white breadcrumbs
½ teaspoon mustard powder
4 tablespoons sesame seeds
salt and freshly ground black pepper
2 eggs
25 g/1 oz plain flour
40 g/1½ oz margarine or butter
4 tablespoons vegetable oil

1 Cut the chicken flesh into strips about 2 cm/¾ inch thick and 7.5 cm/3 inches long.
2 Mix the breadcrumbs, mustard and sesame seeds in a shallow bowl with salt and pepper to taste, then spread out on a flat plate. Beat the eggs in a separate shallow bowl.
3 Put the flour into a polythene bag. Add the chicken strips and shake to coat them evenly. Remove the chicken from the bag and shake off any excess flour. Dip the chicken strips into the beaten egg, then into the breadcrumb mixture until evenly coated.
4 Heat the margarine and oil in a large frying-pan. Add the coated chicken strips and fry for 20 minutes, turning frequently until golden on all sides. (If necessary cook the strips in 2 batches, keeping the cooked batch warm in a low oven.)
5 Remove the strips from the pan with a slotted spoon to a warmed serving dish and serve at once (see Cook's Notes), or leave to drain on absorbent paper and serve cold.

COOK'S NOTES

Preparation takes 30 minutes, cooking time is about 25 minutes.
Chicken breast joints are sold in supermarkets either boneless, or with a small bone in them which is easy to remove. This recipe can also be made with chicken legs.
Serve in an attractive party dish and provide lots of paper napkins so that guests do not get their fingers too greasy.
● 660 calories/2750 kj per portion

72

Surprise terrine

SERVES 6

250 g/9 oz chicken livers
250 g/9 oz boneless belly pork, rind removed
1 small onion, cut into chunks
250 g/9 oz minced beef
1 tablespoon tomato purée
½ teaspoon dried oregano
1 clove garlic, crushed (optional)
3 tablespoons red wine (see Cook's Notes)
salt and freshly ground black pepper
100 g/4 oz stuffed olives
3 bay leaves
1 tablespoon chopped parsley, to garnish

1 Heat the oven to medium temperature, 180C/350F/Gas 4.

2 Wash and trim the livers, removing any discolored parts with a sharp knife.

3 Mince the livers, pork and onion finely in a mincer or chop finely in a food processor (see Cook's Notes). Place in a large bowl and stir in the minced beef, tomato purée, oregano, garlic (if using) and wine. Mix thoroughly and season generously with salt and pepper.

4 Reserve 3 of the olives for garnish, then halve the rest. Spoon half of the terrine mixture into a 700 ml/1¼ pint deep rectangular dish or tin. Arrange the halved olives in the dish (see Cook's Notes).

5 Carefully spoon the remaining terrine mixture on top of the olives and arrange the bay leaves on top. Tap the base of dish a few times on a work surface so the mixture fills the gaps between the olives. Cover the dish loosely with foil.

6 Put the dish into a roasting tin, pour in boiling water to come halfway up the sides of the dish and cook in the oven for about 1½ hours. To see if cooked, tilt the dish and if the juices run clear the terrine is ready. Remove the dish from the roasting tin and cover the surface of the terrine with foil. Put heavy weights on top, leave to cool, then refrigerate overnight.

7 To serve: turn the terrine out on to a platter. Slice the reserved olives and arrange them down the centre of the terrine. Sprinkle a row of chopped parsley on either side.

COOK'S NOTES

The terrine takes about **20 minutes** to prepare, plus **1½ hours cooking time**; it then needs to be left overnight in the refrigerator.

When mincing meats or fish, put a piece of bread into the mincer at the end as it helps to push out the last of the ingredients and their juices.

Use 100 g/4 oz sliced mushrooms instead of the olives. Cook them for 2 minutes in 25 g/1 oz butter before using.

Serve with crusty bread and a fresh green salad for a tasty supper, or serve as a starter on thin toast.

Serve the remaining wine with the terrine, or to be more economical, buy a small bottle of cooking wine concentrate.

● **335 calories/1400 kj per portion**

Mushroom and bacon savouries

MAKES 8

100 g/4 oz mushrooms, finely chopped
8 large rashers back bacon, rinds removed
25 g/1 oz margarine or butter
1 large onion, chopped
50 g/2 oz fresh white breadcrumbs
2 tablespoons finely chopped fresh parsley
½ teaspoon chopped fresh thyme, or ¼ teaspoon dried thyme
½ teaspoon chopped fresh sage, or ¼ teaspoon dried sage
25 g/1 oz shelled walnuts, finely chopped
salt and freshly ground black pepper
2 tablespoons vegetable oil

1 Heat the oven to 190C/375F/ Gas 5.
2 Melt the margarine in a frying-pan, add the onion and fry gently for about 5 minutes until soft.
3 Add the mushrooms to the pan and cook for a further 2 minutes, then remove from heat.
4 Stir the breadcrumbs into the pan with half the parsley, the thyme, sage, walnuts and salt and pepper to taste.
5 Stretch the bacon rashers out on a board and flatten them with the back of a knife.
6 Divide the mushroom mixture into 8 portions. Place a portion on each bacon rasher and roll up like a Swiss roll. Secure the end of each roll with a wooden cocktail stick.
7 Arrange the bacon rolls in a single layer in an ovenproof dish, spoon the oil over evenly, and bake in the oven for 20–25 minutes.
8 Remove the cocktail sticks and arrange the rolls on a warmed serving dish. Sprinkle with the remaining parsley and serve at once.

COOK'S NOTES

Preparation, including pre-cooking, takes about 25 minutes. Cooking in the oven takes 20–25 minutes.
Use only wooden cocktail sticks to secure the rolls: plastic sticks will melt.
Use hazelnuts or peanuts instead of walnuts.
Make double the quantity and serve the hot savouries with canapés at a summer barbecue party.
● 340 calories/1425 kj per portion

Taramasalata

SERVES 8

250 g/9 oz smoked cod's roe
  (see Cook's Notes)
100 g/4 oz sliced white bread, crusts
  removed and soaked in 8 tablespoons water
225 ml/8 fl oz olive oil
1 clove garlic, crushed
4 tablespoons lemon juice
1 tablespoon finely grated onion
  (optional)
freshly ground black pepper
3 tablespoons natural yoghurt
lemon wedges and black olives, to
  garnish

1 Using a sharp knife, carefully peel away the skin from the cod's roe. Alternatively, cut the roe in half and scoop out the inside with a teaspoon.
2 Put the roe in a blender or food processor. Squeeze the excess water from the bread. Add the soaked bread to the cod's roe.
3 Work for a few seconds until smooth. With motor still running, slowly add the olive oil in a thin stream through the hole in the top of the blender goblet, until the mixture is pale pink and creamy (see Cook's Notes).
4 Add the garlic, lemon juice and the onion, if using. Add pepper to taste and work for 1−2 seconds until thoroughly incorporated. Stir in the natural yoghurt, then transfer the pâté to a serving dish, smooth the surface, then cover with cling film and refrigerate for at least 2−3 hours. Garnish with lemon wedges and black olives (see Cook's Notes).

COOK'S NOTES

Preparation takes about 15 minutes. Allow at least 2−3 hours chilling.

Smoked cod's roe is available from most fishmongers and chilling cabinets of large supermarkets. Smoked cod's roe is also available from delicatessens and many super-markets in 65 g/2½ oz jars. You will find you need 2 jars.

The bread may be omitted and 100 g/4 oz cream cheese mixed with 1−2 tablespoons single cream blended with the smoked cod's roe.

Serve taramasalata with slices of warm pitta bread, cubes of French bread or fingers of toast. Present it as part of *mezze*, the Middle Eastern *hors d'oeuvre*, with dishes of olives, lettuce, peppers and cucumber, spring onions, diced Feta cheese and stuffed vine leaves (available in cans from some stores).

Taramasalata gets its name from *tarama*, the Greek word for the salted dried roe of mullet, which was originally used for this pâté. Now-adays smoked cod's roe is almost always used for taramasalata.

● 295 calories/1225 kj per portion

Vegetable samosas

MAKES 12
350 g/12 oz potatoes, diced
250 g/9 oz packet frozen mixed
   vegetables
1 tablespoon vegetable oil
1 onion, finely chopped
1 tablespoon curry powder
6 tablespoons water
salt and freshly ground black pepper
vegetable oil, for deep frying

PASTRY
175 g/6 oz plain flour
salt
25 g/1 oz margarine or butter, diced
about 4 tablespoons water

1 Make the pastry: sift the flour and salt into a bowl. Add the margarine and rub it into the flour with your fingertips until the mixture resembles fine breadcrumbs. Mix in just enough water to make a soft elastic dough. Wrap dough in cling film and refrigerate for 30 minutes.

2 Meanwhile, make the filling: heat the oil in a saucepan, add the onion and fry gently for 5 minutes until soft and lightly coloured.

3 Stir in the curry powder, then add the potatoes and cook for a further 1–2 minutes.

4 Add the mixed vegetables, water and salt and pepper to taste. Bring to the boil, stirring all the time. Lower the heat slightly, cover and simmer for 15–20 minutes, stirring occasionally, until all the vegetables are tender. Allow to cool slightly.

5 Divide the dough into 12 pieces and roll out each piece on a floured surface to a 10 cm/4 inch square.

6 Place 1 tablespoon filling in the centre of each square. Brush the edges of the pastry with water and bring over one corner to form a triangle. Press the sides together and flute.

7 Heat the oil in a deep-fat frier with a basket to 180C/350F or until a day-old bread cube browns in 60 seconds. Put 3 samosas into the basket, then lower into the oil and cook for 2 minutes or until the pastry bubbles and turns golden. Drain on absorbent paper and keep warm while frying the remaining samosas in the same way. Serve at once.

Butter bean dip with crudités

SERVES 8

100 g/4 oz dried butter beans,
  soaked in cold water overnight
  (see Cook's Notes)
4–6 tablespoons good-quality olive
  oil
1 tablespoon red wine vinegar
1 clove garlic, crushed (optional)
salt and freshly ground black pepper

CRUDITÉS

1 small cauliflower, broken into
  florets
1 cucumber, cut into sticks
2 celery stalks, cut into sticks
2 carrots, cut into sticks
1 small green pepper, deseeded and
  cut into strips
1 small red pepper, deseeded and
  cut into strips
bunch of radishes

1 Drain the beans and rinse thoroughly under cold running water. Put them in a large saucepan, cover with fresh cold water and bring to the boil. Lower the heat, half cover with a lid and simmer for about 1½ hours or until the beans are tender. Add more water to the pan during the cooking time if necessary.
2 Drain the beans, reserving the cooking liquid. Put the beans in a blender with 4 tablespoons oil, the vinegar, garlic (if using), a little salt and pepper and 4 tablespoons of the reserved cooking liquid. Blend until thick and smooth, adding a little more liquid if the mixture is too thick.
3 Taste and adjust seasoning, then spoon the mixture into a small bowl and fork over the top; or heap the mixture on a serving plate.
4 Serve the crudités in a shallow basket or salad bowl, or stand the bowl of dip in the centre of a large plate and arrange the crudités around the edge of the plate. If you like, drizzle 2 tablespoons oil over the top of the dip just before serving (see Cook's Notes). Serve at room temperature or refrigerate for about 1 hour before serving.

COOK'S NOTES

Cooking the dried beans takes 1¼ hours and preparing the dip then takes 30 minutes.

If you do not have time to soak the beans in cold water overnight, you can cut down the soaking time considerably by using hot water. Put the beans in a large saucepan, cover with cold water and bring to the boil. Drain and repeat, then remove from the heat and leave to soak in the hot water for 2 hours.

To save even more time, you could use a 425 g/15 oz can butter beans, which are pre-cooked. The whole dip can then be made within 30 minutes.

Dried butter beans can be cooked in a pressure cooker. Soak and rinse as in recipe then cook at high (H) pressure for 20 minutes.

The butter bean dip makes a starter for 8 people.

The dip freezes well, either in the dish from which it will be served or in a rigid container. Store for up to 3 months and allow 2 hours for defrosting at room temperature before serving.

Finishing off the dip with extra oil drizzled on top is usual in Middle Eastern countries, where dips and pâtés made from pulses are very popular. If you do not like too oily a taste, this can be omitted.

● 225 calories/950 kj per portion

Gazpacho

SERVES 4

500 g / 1 lb tomatoes, skinned and coarsely chopped
½ cucumber, peeled and coarsely chopped
1 green pepper, deseeded and coarsely chopped
1 small onion, coarsely chopped
1 clove garlic, chopped
2 slices white bread, crusts removed, crumbled
1 teaspoon salt, or to taste
2 tablespoons red wine vinegar
1 L / 1¾ pints iced water
5 tablespoons olive oil

GARNISHES

2 slices bread, crusts removed, and cubed
4 tablespoons olive oil
2 eggs, hard-boiled and chopped
½ cucumber, peeled and finely chopped
1 small green pepper, deseeded and finely chopped
1 onion, finely diced

1 In a large bowl, combine the tomatoes, cucumber, green pepper, onion, garlic, bread, salt and vinegar. Add the water and mix thoroughly (see Cook's Notes). Purée the mixture in a food processor or blender until smooth. Return the purée to the bowl and whisk in the oil in a thin, steady stream. Cover the bowl with cling film and refrigerate for about 2 hours until thoroughly chilled.

2 To make the croûtons: heat the oil in a heavy frying-pan over moderate heat until very hot, add the bread cubes and fry until golden brown on all sides, turning them frequently. Drain on absorbent paper and put into a small serving bowl.

3 Put the eggs, cucumber, green pepper and onion into separate small serving bowls.

4 When the soup is well chilled, stir thoroughly and taste and adjust seasoning. Pour into 4 chilled individual soup bowls and serve the garnishes separately presented in individual bowls.

COOK'S NOTES

Preparation takes about 45 minutes, but remember that the soup needs to be chilled for about 2 hours.

Do not forget to stir the soup just before serving.

If the tomatoes have a poor colour, add some tomato purée to the ingredients before you purée them.

● 370 calories / 1550 kj per portion

Avocado dip

SERVES 4–6
2 ripe avocados (see Cook's Notes)
juice of 1 lemon
1 clove garlic, crushed (optional)
4 tomatoes, skinned, deseeded and
finely chopped
1 small onion, finely chopped
4 tablespoons finely chopped celery
2–3 tablespoons olive oil
1 tablespoon chopped fresh parsley
salt and freshly ground black pepper

1 Cut the avocados in half length-ways (see Cook's Notes), remove the stones then scoop out the flesh with a teaspoon. Put the flesh in a bowl and mash it with a wooden spoon.
2 Add the lemon juice, garlic (if using), tomatoes, onion and celery.
3 Stir in enough olive oil to make a soft, smooth mixture, then add the chopped parsley and season with salt and pepper to taste.
4 Transfer the dip to a serving bowl, cover with cling film and chill in the refrigerator for about 30 minutes. Serve chilled.

COOK'S NOTES

This dip takes 20 minutes prepara-tion, then 30 minutes chilling.

Avocados are ripe when the flesh at the rounded end yields slightly when gently pressed. Reject any avocados that are hard or very soft or have blotched, dry skins.

When cutting the avocado, use a stainless steel knife to prevent the avocado flesh from discoloring at the beginning.

Serve with a selection of small crackers, potato crisps or crisp raw vegetables.
● 325 calories/1350 kj per portion

SIDE DISHES & SALADS

Pulse-filled pittas

SERVES 4
250 g/9 oz split red lentils
40 g/1½ oz margarine or butter
1 onion, finely chopped
100 g/4 oz button mushrooms,
  thinly sliced
2 teaspoons ground cumin
450 ml/16 fl oz chicken or ham
  stock
2 tablespoons lemon juice
1 tablespoon finely chopped fresh
  parsley
salt and freshly ground black pepper
4 white or brown pitta breads
4 tomatoes, thinly sliced

1 Melt the margarine in a saucepan. Add the onion and fry gently for 3–4 minutes until soft but not coloured. Add the mushrooms and cumin and fry for a further 2 minutes, stirring.

2 Add the lentils and stock to the pan and bring to the boil, then turn down the heat to very low. Cover and simmer for 20–30 minutes, stirring occasionally until the lentils are soft and the liquid has been absorbed.
3 Add the lemon juice and parsley and season to taste with salt and pepper. Keep warm over low heat, stirring occasionally until the mixture is really thick.
4 Light the barbecue.
5 When the coals are hot, dampen the pitta breads by sprinkling them all over with cold water, then toast them (see Cook's Notes) for about 2–3 minutes on each side, until just crisp. Cut them in half, horizontally, and ease open with a round-bladed knife. Divide the lentil mixture between the pitta 'pockets' and slip a few tomato slices into each one.

COOK'S NOTES

Total preparation and cooking time for this wholefood snack is about 50 minutes.

Fold a paper napkin around each filled pitta, so that it can be eaten in the hand.

Serve with a Greek-style salad made with shredded lettuce or white cabbage, sliced tomatoes, cucumber and a few black olives. Crumbled or cubed Greek Feta cheese makes a tasty topping to this salad; or Caerphilly or Lancashire cheese can be used as an alternative if Feta is difficult to obtain.

Dampening the pitta breads keeps them soft and prevents them becoming dry and cracked when toasted. If cut in half, they can be toasted in an automatic 'pop-up' toaster for speed.

● **495 calories/2075 kj per portion**

Devilled corn
on the cob

SERVES 4

4 corn on the cob (see Cook's Notes)
75 g/3 oz butter, softened
4 tablespoons tomato ketchup
½ teaspoon Worcestershire sauce
1–2 tablespoons finely snipped
   chives

1 Light the barbecue.
2 Put the softened butter in a small bowl and, using a fork, blend in the tomato ketchup, Worcestershire sauce and snipped chives. Beat until well combined.
3 Remove the husks and silky threads from the corn on the cob (see Cook's Notes). Bring a large saucepan of unsalted water to the boil. Put in the corn on the cob, bring back to the boil and cook for 6 minutes. Drain well.
4 Place each corn on the cob on a piece of heavy-duty foil about 30 cm/12 inches square, and spread with the butter mixture. Bring the edges of the foil together over each corn on the cob and crimp them securely together, to make a parcel.
5 When the coals are hot place the foil parcels in amongst them and cook for 15–20 minutes, turning several times. Remove from the foil and transfer to warmed serving plates with the buttery juices poured over.

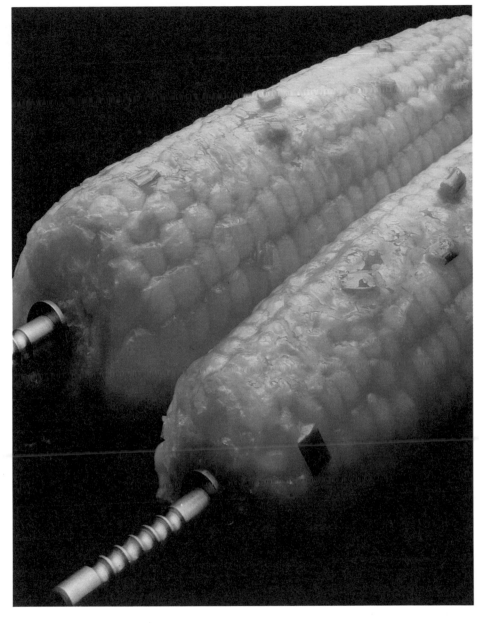

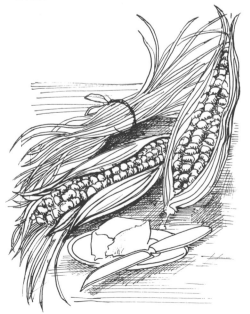

COOK'S NOTES

Preparation time is 20 minutes and cooking time is 20 minutes.

When corn on the cob is out of season, you can use frozen corn on the cob, which is available in most large supermarkets. Put the frozen cobs in boiling water, bring back to the boil, then drain at once, place on the squares of foil and spread with the butter mixture.

Never cook corn on the cob in salted water as this toughens the kernels.

Use finely chopped parsley instead of finely snipped chives in the butter mixture.

Serve Devilled corn on the cob on its own as a vegetable starter, or it could accompany a main dish. Provide plenty of paper napkins for wiping buttery fingers.

For ease of serving, there are specially-designed corn on the cob holders available. These are skewered into either end of the cob, so that you can grip the cob firmly without burning your fingers.

● 235 calories/1000 kj per portion

Potato and radish crunch

SERVES 4
500 g/1 lb new potatoes
salt
50 g/2 oz butter
3 thick slices white bread, crusts removed and cut into 1 cm/ ½ inch dice
5 cm/2 inch piece of cucumber, diced
6 radishes, thinly sliced
25 g/1 oz dry roasted peanuts
1 teaspoon snipped chives
freshly ground black pepper
4 tablespoons soured cream

1 Boil a saucepan of salted water and cook the potatoes for 15–20 minutes until just tender.
2 Drain well and, when cool enough to handle, cut into 1 cm/½ inch dice. Leave to cool completely.
3 To make the croûtons: melt the butter in a frying-pan. When it is sizzling, add the diced bread and fry gently, turning as necessary, until golden.
4 Drain well on absorbent paper. Leave to cool completely.
5 Place the diced potato, fried croûtons, cucumber, radishes, peanuts and chives in a bowl.
6 Season to taste with salt and pepper. Add the soured cream and mix gently. Serve at once.

COOK'S NOTES

Preparation, including cooking the potatoes and frying the croûtons, takes about 30 minutes. Allow 30 minutes for cooling. Preparing the salad takes 5 minutes.

Choose a waxy type of potato such as Pentland Javelin or Ulster Sceptre which will not break up during cooking.

Watch the potatoes carefully: they should be cooked through but still firm. If overcooked, they will break up instead of cutting into neat dice.

Mix gently so that the ingredients are thoroughly coated in the soured cream but remain separate.

Add a small chopped green pepper instead of cucumber.

Omit the peanuts and sprinkle the top of the salad with toasted, flaked almonds.

● 310 calories/1300 kj per portion

Lentil salad

SERVES 6
500 g/1 lb whole brown lentils,
    washed and drained
1 medium onion, halved
1 medium carrot, halved
2 celery stalks, halved
1 bay leaf
salt

DRESSING
3 tablespoons vegetable oil
1 tablespoon lemon juice
½ teaspoon dried mixed herbs
freshly ground black pepper
2–3 spring onions, finely chopped
2 celery stalks, thinly sliced
2 tablespoons chopped parsley
parsley sprigs and 1 lemon,
    quartered, to garnish

1 Put the lentils into a large saucepan with the onion, carrot, celery and bay leaf and cover with water. Bring to the boil, then lower the heat, cover and simmer gently for about 1 hour, or until the lentils are tender but not mushy. Check occasionally and add more boiling water if necessary. Add salt just before the end of cooking time.
2 Meanwhile, make the dressing: mix together the oil and lemon juice, stir in the mixed herbs and season well with salt and pepper.
3 Strain the lentils, discarding the liquid, vegetables and bay leaf, and turn the lentils into a bowl.
4 Immediately pour over the dressing and mix to blend thoroughly without breaking up the lentils. Stir in the spring onions and celery with the chopped parsley.
5 Allow to cool, cover the bowl, then chill in the refrigerator for about 2 hours.
6 Turn the lentil salad into a serving dish, and garnish with parsley sprigs and lemon or serve with a salad.

COOK'S NOTES

Preparation and cooking the lentils take about 1½ hours. Allow a further 2 hours for chilling.

This substantial salad is good with any cold roast meat, especially beef and ham. It can also be served as part of a vegetarian meal, with tomato or cucumber salads.

Pour the dressing over the lentils while they are hot so that it will be absorbed easily.

Add a little spice to the salad by replacing the herbs in the dressing with 1½ teaspoons mild curry powder.
● 320 calories/1350 kj per portion

Chick-pea salad

SERVES 4
100 g/4 oz chick-peas
3 tablespoons olive oil
1 tablespoon wine vinegar
salt and fresh ground black pepper
500 g/1 lb tomatoes, skinned and
   sliced
1 medium onion, thinly sliced
2 teaspoons freshly chopped basil,
   or 1 teaspoon dried basil

1 Put the chick-peas into a deep bowl, cover with plenty of cold water and leave to soak for 8 hours.
2 Drain the chick-peas, rinse under cold running water, then put them into a saucepan and cover with fresh cold water. Bring to the boil, then reduce heat and simmer for about 1 hour until tender. Add more water during cooking if necessary.
3 Drain the cooked chick-peas and leave to cool.
4 Put the oil and vinegar into a bowl. Mix together with a fork, and season to taste with salt and pepper. Add the chick-peas and mix gently until well coated with dressing. Take care not to break them up.
5 Lay the tomato and onion slices in a shallow serving dish and sprinkle with the basil and salt and pepper to taste. Spoon the dressed chick-peas over the top. Serve cold.

COOK'S NOTES

Preparation takes 15 minutes, plus 8 hours soaking, then 1 hour cooking for the chick-peas.

Preparation time is greatly reduced by using a 425 g/15 oz can chick-peas, well drained and rinsed.

Chick-peas are rich in protein and widely used in stews and other traditional dishes in Spain, India and the Middle East.

Chick-peas can be cooked in a pressure cooker. Soak and rinse as in the recipe, then cook at high (H) pressure for 20 minutes.

This nourishing salad goes very well with barbecued food and can be served with soft wholemeal rolls or warm pitta bread.

For a dinner party, serve the salad as a fairly substantial starter, provided the main course is light.

Chick-peas freeze well after soaking and cooking. After cooling, freeze in rigid containers for up to 2 months. Allow several hours for defrosting at room temperature.

With the increased interest in healthy wholefoods, dried chick-peas are available from most supermarkets as well as specialist health food stores and Asian food shops.
● 195 calories/825 kj per portion

Sweetcorn, radish and apple salad

SERVES 4

500 g/1 lb frozen sweetcorn kernels
1 bunch radishes, thinly sliced
  (see Cook's Notes)
2 crisp green dessert apples
  (see Cook's Notes)
1 tablespoon lemon juice

DRESSING

3 tablespoons vegetable oil
1 tablespoon wine vinegar
1 teaspoon sugar
1 teaspoon mustard powder
salt and freshly ground black pepper

1 Cook the sweetcorn according to packet instructions. Drain and cool.
2 Core and dice the apples, then put in a bowl and sprinkle with the lemon juice. Toss to coat well.
3 Make the dressing: put the dressing ingredients into a salad bowl with salt and pepper to taste and mix together with a fork.
4 Add the sweetcorn, apples and radishes to the dressing and stir gently until mixed. Serve at once.

COOK'S NOTES

It takes 25 minutes to make this salad.

An average bunch of small radishes will weigh about 100 g/4 oz. Extra large radishes, when available, can be used instead of small ones..Granny Smith apples are the best choice for this recipe.

Try using a bunch of finely chopped spring onions, instead of the apples, and omit the lemon juice.

● 230 calories/950 kj per portion

Endive and bacon salad

SERVES 4

1 large endive, leaves separated
4 tablespoons vegetable oil
1 clove garlic, crushed
2 slices stale white bread, 1 cm/
  ½ inch thick, crusts removed, cut
  into cubes
175 g/6 oz lean bacon, rinds
  removed, chopped
2 tablespoons wine vinegar
salt and freshly ground black pepper

1 Heat the oven to 110C/225F/ Gas ¼. Place the endive in a salad bowl.

2 Heat 2 tablespoons of the oil in a heavy-based frying-pan, add the garlic and fry gently for 1–2 minutes or until soft and lightly coloured. Using a slotted spoon, remove and discard the garlic.

3 Add the cubes of bread and fry for 5 minutes over moderate heat, stirring to prevent sticking, until they are crisp and golden brown. Remove with a slotted spoon, drain on absorbent paper and keep hot in the oven.

4 Heat the remaining oil in the frying-pan, add the bacon and fry over moderate heat for about 5 minutes until crisp. Stir in the vinegar, then immediately pour over the endive.

5 Sprinkle over the fried bread cubes and salt and pepper to taste, then toss well and serve at once.

COOK'S NOTES

Total preparation time is 20 minutes.

Do not allow the salad to stand before serving; the dressing and bread must be hot when the salad is served.

Serve with chunks of crusty bread as a first course. Alternatively, serve as a side salad to roast or grilled meat or poultry.

● 325 calories/1375 kj per portion

Tangy potato salad

SERVES 6

500 g/1 lb potatoes, cut into even-
   sized chunks (see Cook's Notes)
salt
175 ml/6 fl oz thick bottled
   mayonnaise
1 tablespoon olive oil
1 tablespoon grated fresh
   horseradish (see Cook's Notes)
freshly ground black pepper
½ teaspoon sweet paprika
1 teaspoon finely chopped fresh
   parsley

1 Put the potato chunks in a large saucepan; cover with cold water, add a pinch of salt and bring to the boil. Lower the heat slightly and simmer for 20–25 minutes until the potatoes are tender.

2 Meanwhile, put the mayonnaise into a large serving bowl and stir in the olive oil, horseradish and salt and pepper to taste.

3 Drain the potatoes and leave to cool slightly for about 10 minutes.

4 Add the potatoes to the mayonnaise, carefully turning them to ensure that all the pieces are evenly coated. Leave to stand for 1 hour.

5 Just before serving, sprinkle over the paprika and parsley.

COOK'S NOTES

This salad takes 15 minutes preparation, 20–30 minutes cooking, plus 1 hour 10 minutes standing.

Do not allow the potatoes to become completely cold before adding them to the mayonnaise otherwise the flavours will not blend so well. On the other hand, they should not be added while still very hot or the mayonnaise may curdle. Buy a waxy potato such as Desirée.

Fresh horseradish is available from most good greengrocers. If unobtainable, however, substitute 2–3 teaspoons horseradish sauce.

● 270 calories/1125 kj per portion

87

Two-bean salad

SERVES 4
**100 g/4 oz dried red kidney beans,
   soaked overnight**
**100 g/4 oz dried haricot beans,
   soaked overnight**
1 small onion, chopped
1 bay leaf
2 large celery stalks, thinly sliced
1 green pepper, deseeded and diced

DRESSING
6 tablespoons olive oil
2 tablespoons wine vinegar
1 clove garlic, crushed (optional)
salt and freshly ground black pepper

1 Drain the kidney beans, transfer to a saucepan, cover with water and bring to the boil. Boil vigorously for 10 minutes, then add the haricot beans, together with their soaking liquid. Add the onion and bay leaf and bring back to the boil. Reduce the heat slightly, half cover with a lid and simmer for about 1 hour until the beans are tender.

2 Meanwhile, make the dressing: put the ingredients in a screw-top jar, with salt and pepper to taste. Replace the lid firmly and shake well to mix.

3 Drain the beans and discard the cooking liquid and bay leaf. Transfer to a serving dish and pour over the dressing, while the beans are still warm (see Cook's Notes).

4 Mix well, cover and refrigerate for at least 1 hour or preferably overnight.

5 Add the celery and diced pepper to the beans, taste and adjust seasoning and mix well. Serve.

COOK'S NOTES

Allow 10 minutes preparation then 1¼ hours cooking and at least 1 hour standing time.

This salad is ideal for serving with cold meats. To serve it as a starter for 6, arrange on individual plates lined with lettuce leaves and garnish with hard-boiled egg.

The kidney beans must be boiled vigorously for a good 10 minutes before simmering, to remove poisonous elements.

The beans will absorb more flavour if they are still warm when dressed.

● 330 calories/1375 kj per portion

Crunchy mixed salad

SERVES 4
¼ **large cucumber**
275 g/10 oz beansprouts (see Cook's
   Notes)
175 g/6 oz **green grapes**
1 **small onion, thinly sliced**

DRESSING
50 g/2 oz **Lancashire cheese**
2 **tablespoons vegetable oil**
1 **tablespoon white wine vinegar**
½ **teaspoon French mustard**
¼ **teaspoon sugar**
salt and freshly ground black pepper

1 Peel the cucumber, cut it in half lengthways, then scoop out the seeds (see Cook's Notes). Cut into matchstick strips about 5 cm/2 inches long and pat dry on absorbent paper.

2 Wash the beansprouts under cold running water, trim off any roots and drain well on absorbent paper.

3 Cut the grapes in half, or quarter them if large, and remove the pips with the point of a sharp knife.

4 Make the dressing: crumble the cheese finely into a large bowl. Whisk in the oil, vinegar, mustard, sugar and salt and pepper to taste.

5 Add the cucumber, beansprouts, onion and grapes to the dressing and toss well to combine. Cover and leave to stand for 10 minutes to allow the flavours to blend.

6 Just before serving, toss the salad to gather up the juices.

COOK'S NOTES

Preparation takes about 40 minutes, including standing time.

The salad goes well with canned fish such as pilchards, tuna or mackerel.

Beansprouts are often sold in supermarkets in 275 g/10 oz packets. Eat beansprouts within 2 days of buying.

Removing the cucumber seeds helps to reduce the moisture which can dilute salad dressing.

● 155 calories/650 kj per portion

Thousand island salad

SERVES 4–6

250 g/9 oz boneless cooked
  chicken, diced
250 g/9 oz thickly sliced ham, diced
250 g/9 oz mature Cheddar cheese,
  diced
freshly ground black pepper
½ small iceberg or crisp lettuce
2 carrots, thinly sliced (see Cook's
  Notes)
¼ cucumber, thinly sliced
1 red or green pepper, deseeded and
  thinly sliced
watercress, to garnish (optional)

THOUSAND ISLAND DRESSING

150 ml/¼ pint thick bottled
  mayonnaise
1 hard boiled egg
8 stuffed olives, finely chopped
¼ green pepper, finely chopped
2 teaspoons finely chopped fresh
  parsley
2 teaspoons finely chopped onion
2 teaspoons tomato purée
¼ teaspoon sweet paprika
1 teaspoon lemon juice
good pinch of chilli seasoning

1 Prepare the dressing: put the
mayonnaise in a bowl. Reserve the
egg white and press the egg yolk
through a sieve. Add to the mayonnaise. Stir the remaining dressing
ingredients into the mayonnaise and
mix so that they are thoroughly
blended.
2 Put the chicken, ham and cheese
in a bowl. Season well with black
pepper and mix the ingredients
together.
3 Divide the lettuce into 4 and
arrange in the base of 4 individual
salad bowls.
4 Divide the chicken mixture into
4 and pile into the centre of each
bowl. Mix together the sliced carrots,
cucumber, and pepper and sprinkle
a little over the top of each salad.
Chop the reserved egg white and
sprinkle a little over each bowl, then
garnish with sprigs of watercress, if
liked. Serve at once.

COOK'S NOTES

The salad and dressing take about
40 minutes to prepare and arrange.
  Store any left-over dressing in a
screw-top jar in the refrigerator to
serve with other salads.
  Omit the ham and use instead
2 varieties of cheese such as Red
Leicester and Lancashire.
  Serve smaller portions as a tasty
starter or serve this substantial
salad with barbecued meat or fish.
● 740 calories/3100 kj per portion

Mixed salad with hot dressing

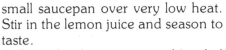

SERVES 4–6

1 crisp lettuce (see Cook's Notes)
250 g/9 oz radishes
250 g/9 oz peas, unshelled weight
(see Cook's Notes)

DRESSING
100 g/4 oz butter
1 tablespoon lemon juice
salt and freshly ground black pepper

1 Roughly tear up the lettuce and put into a salad bowl.
2 Slice the radishes and add them to the lettuce together with the shelled peas.
3 Make the dressing: melt butter in a small saucepan over very low heat. Stir in the lemon juice and season to taste.
4 Pour the dressing on to the salad while it is still warm. Toss the salad with dressing and serve at once.

COOK'S NOTES

This summery salad only takes about 10 minutes to make.

An unusual combination of a hot dressing with cold vegetables, this makes an excellent side salad. It is especially good with chicken and fish dishes.

If liked, garnish with sprinkling of crumbled, crisply-fried bacon or bread croûtons fried in butter, oil and garlic.

This quantity of unshelled peas will produce about 100 g/4 oz peas after shelling. If fresh peas are unavailable, use 100 g/4 oz defrosted frozen peas.

Serve the salad immediately, otherwise the hot dressing will make the lettuce go limp very quickly.

● 220 calories/925 kj per portion

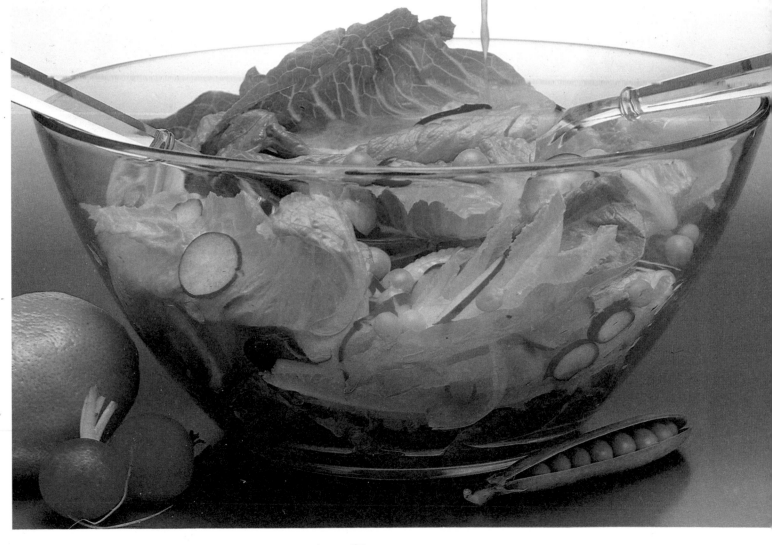

Green and gold salad

SERVES 4
1 lettuce, leaves separated
2 carrots, cut into small matchstick
 pieces
¼ cucumber, thinly sliced
2 avocado pears
1 tablespoon lemon juice
300 g/11 oz can mandarin orange
 segments

DRESSING
6 tablespoons thick bottled
 mayonnaise
1 teaspoon ground turmeric
2 teaspoons sweet chutney, finely
 chopped

1 Line 4 individual plates with the
lettuce leaves.
2 Garnish each plate with a border
of carrots and cucumber.
3 Halve, stone and peel avocados,
then slice them both lengthways (see
Cook's Notes). Immediately sprinkle
them with lemon juice to prevent
discoloration, then arrange on the
plates, on top of the cucumber slices.
4 Drain the mandarins, reserving
1 tablespoon of syrup for the dressing. Pile a spoonful of mandarin
oranges in the centre of each plate,
reserving 4 segments for garnish.
5 Make the dressing: put the
mayonnaise in a bowl and stir in
the reserved mandarin syrup, the
turmeric and chutney. Mix all the
ingredients well.
6 Spoon a little dressing over each
portion of mandarins, then garnish
with a mandarin segment.
7 Serve the green and gold salad
at once, with any of the remaining
dressing handed in a jug, separately.

COOK'S NOTES

This attractive salad takes about
30 minutes to make, including the
preparation of the vegetables.
 Peel the avocados as thinly as
possible to keep the attractive dark
green colour on the outside.
 Although the avocados are
sprinkled with lemon juice, it is best
to prepare them as near to serving
time as possible to ensure that they
do not become discoloured.
 If preferred, replace the mandarins with 3 oranges, cut into
segments. When peeling the
oranges, catch 1 tablespoon of the
juice for use in the dressing.
 Use remaining syrup in a fruit
salad or jelly.
 Serve as a refreshing starter, or as
a colourful side salad with grilled
fish or lamb cutlets.
● 385 calories/1600 kj per portion

Pasta salad

SERVES 4

250 g/9 oz green tagliatelle
salt
45 g/1¾ oz can anchovy fillets, drained and soaked in milk for 20 minutes
225 g/8 oz Cheddar cheese, finely diced
2 tomatoes, skinned and thickly sliced
2 celery stalks, chopped
8 black olives, halved and stoned
2 tablespoons grated Parmesan cheese

DRESSING

3 tablespoons vegetable oil
1 tablespoon wine vinegar
½ teaspoon mustard powder
freshly ground black pepper

1 Cook the tagliatelle in boiling salted water (see Cook's Notes) for 5–10 minutes until just tender. Drain thoroughly, then rinse well under cold running water, to remove any excess starch from the pasta.

2 While the pasta is cooking, make the dressing: combine the oil, vinegar, mustard and salt and pepper to taste in a screw-top jar. Shake the jar well until all the ingredients in the dressing are thoroughly blended.

3 Drain the anchovy fillets and pat dry with absorbent paper. Put them into a bowl with cooked tagliatelle, cheese, tomatoes, celery and olives, then pour in the dressing. Toss gently, until all the salad ingredients are evenly coated.

4 Pile the salad on to a serving dish and sprinkle with Parmesan.

COOK'S NOTES

This salad takes about 20 minutes, including the cooking of the tagliatelle.

To prevent pasta sticking together while cooking, add 2 drops of vegetable oil to the water.

Other pasta shapes, such as shells or butterflies, can be used.

It is very important not to overcook the pasta, or the salad will be stodgy.

● 600 calories/2500 kj per portion

Sweet and sour salad

SERVES 4

½ teaspoon hot curry powder
150 g/5 oz natural yoghurt
1 tablespoon chutney (see Cook's Notes)
salt and freshly ground black pepper
1 small head celery, sliced (see Cook's Notes)
100 g/4 oz Cheshire cheese, crumbled
50 g/2 oz stoned dates, sliced
2 crisp dessert apples

1 Beat the curry powder into the yoghurt, then stir in the chutney, season well with salt and pepper and set aside.

2 Toss together the celery, cheese and dates. Core and chop the apples and add to the other ingredients.

3 Pour the yoghurt dressing over the salad and fork through lightly until all the ingredients are evenly coated. Taste and adjust seasoning. Serve as soon as possible.

COOK'S NOTES

The salad takes about 20 minutes to prepare.

Half a crisp white cabbage, finely shredded, or 2 heads of chicory can replace the celery.

Use 2 small oranges, segmented with all the pith removed, instead of the apples and 50 g/2 oz sultanas or seedless raisins in place of the dates.

Substitute another white, crumbly cheese such as Lancashire or Wensleydale for the Cheshire.

Mayonnaise can be used instead of natural yoghurt.

Use an apple-based chutney in the dressing for this salad.

Celery should be stored in a cool place, ideally in the salad compartment of the refrigerator. It is possible to crisp up celery which has become a little limp by plunging it in iced water or washing it in cold water and putting it in the coldest part of the refrigerator.

As the cheese is crumbled, this is a good recipe for using up cheese which has become crumbly in the freezer.

Use the trimmings from the celery to flavour soups or casseroles. Or infuse it in the warmed milk for making a white sauce, especially to serve with fish.

Sprinkle 2 tablespoons chopped peanuts, walnuts or almonds over the surface of the salad for a crunchy and attractive garnish.

● 190 calories/800 kj per portion

Brussels sprouts and date salad

SERVES 6
500 g/1 lb Brussels sprouts
250 g/9 oz carrots, grated
100 g/4 oz stoned dates, chopped

DRESSING
150 g/5 oz natural yoghurt, chilled
2 tablespoons mayonnaise
2 tablespoons fresh orange juice
salt and freshly ground black pepper
2 tablespoons snipped chives

TO SERVE
2 heads chicory or 1 lettuce heart,
trimmed and separated into leaves
25 g/1 oz walnut halves (optional)

1 Trim the sprouts, discarding any tough or discolored outer leaves. Wash and drain them thoroughly, tossing them in a clean tea-towel or on absorbent paper.
2 Shred the sprouts with a sharp knife, then place in a large mixing bowl with the grated carrots and dates. Mix well to combine.
3 To make the dressing: beat together the yoghurt, mayonnaise and orange juice. Add salt and pepper to taste, then stir in the chives.
4 Pour the dressing over the vegetables and mix well. Taste and adjust seasoning. Cover and refrigerate for about 1 hour, or longer.
5 To serve: line a deep serving bowl

with the chicory or lettuce leaves, then spoon the chilled salad into the centre, piling it up in a mound. Garnish with the walnuts, if using.

COOK'S NOTES

There is 45 minutes preparation, plus at least 1 hour chilling to make this unusual salad.

This unusual salad has a slightly 'tangy' flavour, and makes a refreshing first course. It is also a good accompaniment to barbecued meat.

Use 2 tablespoons each seedless raisins and sultanas instead of the dates.

● **145 calories/600 kj per portion**

Green salad with peanut dressing

SERVES 4

1 small cos lettuce, cut crossways
   into 8 slices (see Cook's Notes)
1 bunch watercress, separated
1 small cucumber, finely diced
   (see Cook's Notes)
50 g/2 oz seedless raisins
25 g/1 oz unsalted peanuts

DRESSING

1 tablespoon peanut butter
6 tablespoons vegetable oil
2 tablespoons cider or wine vinegar
pinch of caster sugar
salt and freshly ground black pepper

1 Put the sliced cos lettuce and watercress sprigs, together with the finely diced cucumber, in a large salad bowl.
2 To make the dressing: put the peanut butter in a bowl and then gradually beat in the oil a little at a time until the mixture is smooth and glossy. Beat in the vinegar and sugar until well blended and season to taste with salt and pepper (see Cook's Notes).
3 Just before serving, add the raisins and peanuts to the salad ingredients in the bowl.
4 Pour the dressing over the salad and, using 2 large forks or salad servers, toss until all the ingredients are well coated with dressing and glistening. Serve the salad at once, while the ingredients are still crisp.

COOK'S NOTES

Salad preparation takes about 15 minutes.
   Crisp lettuce like cos is ideal for a salad with a heavy dressing: the leaves do not become limp.
   There is no need to peel the cucumber: dicing it finely helps make it more digestible.
   You can make the salad dressing well in advance and store it in the refrigerator in a screw-top jar.
● 125 calories/525 kj per portion

SUMMER DESSERTS

Blackberry mousse

SERVES 6

750 g/1½ lb blackberries, fresh or
   frozen (see Cook's Notes)
75 g/3 oz caster sugar
4 tablespoons water
1½ rounded tablespoons
   (1½ sachets) gelatine
150 ml/¼ pint double cream
2 egg whites

1 Reserve a few whole blackberries for decoration, then put the remainder in a saucepan. Add the sugar, cover and cook gently until soft and mushy, stirring occasionally. Press the cooked blackberries through a nylon sieve (see Cook's Notes).
2 Put the water in a small bowl, sprinkle the gelatine over the top and leave to soak for about 5 minutes until spongy. Stand the bowl in a pan of gently simmering water and stir until the gelatine has dissolved and the liquid is clear.
3 Remove the bowl from the pan and cool slightly. Pour the gelatine solution in a thin stream on to the sieved blackberries, stirring constantly. Allow to cool then refrigerate until beginning to set.
4 Whip the cream until thick and fold into the cooled purée.
5 Whisk the egg whites until they stand in stiff peaks and fold into the mixture. Pour into a serving dish, or into 6 individual glasses, and refrigerate for at least 4 hours until set.
6 Just before serving, decorate with the reserved blackberries for that finishing touch.

COOK'S NOTES

Allow 30 minutes preparation, plus cooling and about 4 hours chilling time.
   The blackberries must be sieved rather than puréed in a blender, or food processor, in order to remove the woody pips.
   Serve with sponge finger biscuits or shortbread fingers to provide a contrast in texture.
   Open freeze the mousse until solid, then cover with cling film and wrap in a polythene bag. Seal, label and return to the freezer for up to 3 months. To serve: defrost in the refrigerator for at least 4 hours.
   There is no need to defrost frozen blackberries before cooking with the sugar.
● 210 calories/875 kj per portion

Special fruit sundaes

SERVES 4

finely grated zest and juice of ½ lime
400 g/14 oz can figs, drained, with
    syrup reserved
caster sugar, to taste
2 kiwi fruits
1 large pear
50 g/2 oz fresh dates (see Cook's
    Notes)
1 large banana
crisp biscuits, to serve

1 Measure the lime juice, then add enough of the reserved fig syrup to make up to 100 ml/3½ fl oz. Stir in the lime zest and caster sugar to taste.
2 Pour into a small, heavy-based saucepan, bring to the boil and boil, without stirring, for 2 minutes. Pour the syrup into a heatproof jug and then leave the mixture to cool for about 15 minutes.
3 Meanwhile, peel and slice the kiwi fruits and place in a bowl. Slice any large figs in half lengthways, then add to the bowl. Peel, quarter, core and slice the pear and add to the bowl together with the prepared dates.
4 Strain the lime and syrup mixture over the fruits, then mix gently together. Cover with cling film and refrigerate for at least 1 hour, or up to 6 hours.
5 To serve: slice the banana into the fruits and mix gently. Divide the fruits and syrup between 4 sundae or other stemmed glass dishes. Serve chilled, with a plate of crisp biscuits handed around separately.

COOK'S NOTES

Preparation takes 30 minutes, plus at least 1 hour chilling time.

The syrup mixture should taste slightly sharp, as both the dates and figs are high in sugar and will add extra sweetness.

Use a flexible spatula or your fingers to turn the fruits very gently; this will avoid breaking them.

Prepare fresh dates as follows: using a small sharp knife, make a small slit in the paper brown skin, at the stalk end. With your fingers, gently squeeze out the date. Cut the date in half lengthways and ease out the stone.

If fresh dates are difficult to obtain, use 6 whole dried dates: skin, halve and stone them before adding to the bowl.

You can serve this most unusual and delicious blend of chilled fruits accompanied by ice cream.

● 240 calories/1245 kj per portion

Melon fruit salads

SERVES 4

2 small melons (see Cook's Notes)
1 mango, thickly sliced and cut into cubes
300 g/11 oz can mandarin orange segments, drained
1 tablespoon frozen concentrated orange juice, defrosted
250 g/9 oz raspberries, hulled
caster sugar and soured cream, to serve

1 Prepare the melons (see Cook's Notes), reserving the trimmings. Wrap the melons in polythene bags, seal and chill until required.
2 Trim the flesh from the melon trimmings and place in a bowl with the mango. Add the mandarin segments and orange juice and stir the fruits gently to mix. Cover the bowl with cling film and chill in the refrigerator for at least 1 hour.
3 To assemble: drain any juice from the melons, then place them on 4 dessert plates. Drain the other fruits well, then gently stir in the raspberries. Pile the mixture into the melons. Leave to stand at room temperature for a few minutes before serving to take the chill off. Hand a bowl of caster sugar and a jug of soured cream to all the guests separately.

COOK'S NOTES

Allow 40 minutes preparation, plus at least 1 hour chilling time.

Charentais or small cantaloupe melons are the perfect size for this dessert, and their sweet, orangy-coloured flesh blends beautifully with the other fruits. If neither is available, use green-fleshed ogen melons instead.

Ripe melons feel heavy for their size and the end opposite the stalk will 'give' slightly if gently pressed. At their peak, charentais and cantaloupe melons have a strong, musky scent.

Small melons make attractive edible containers for fruit salads.

(The melon flesh is eaten when the filling is finished.) To prepare: trim off the stalk, then cut the melons horizontally in half. Scrape out the seeds and membrane. Cut small 'V' shaped wedges around the cut edges of each melon half to give a waterlily effect. Drain any juice from the cavity.

Once cut, melon must be tightly wrapped or its scent will permeate other foods in the refrigerator.

Do not add the raspberries until ready to assemble the salad, or their colour will run and spoil its appearance.

● 155 calories/650 kj per portion

Soured cream cheesecake

SERVES 10–12
**250 g/9 oz digestive biscuits,
   crushed (see Cook's Notes)
100 g/4 oz finely chopped hazelnuts
100 g/4 oz butter, melted
margarine, for greasing**

FILLING
**500 g/1 lb Philadelphia cream
   cheese
3 large eggs
100 g/4 oz caster sugar
½ teaspoon vanilla flavouring
1 teaspoon grated lemon zest**

TOPPING
**425 ml/¾ pint soured cream
100 g/4 oz caster sugar
1 teaspoon vanilla flavouring**

1 Heat the oven to 180C/350F/ Gas 4. Grease the base of a deep 23 cm/9 inch loose-bottomed cake tin with margarine and line with a circle of greaseproof paper.
2 Mix the crushed biscuits, chopped hazelnuts and melted butter in a bowl. Then press the mixture evenly over the base of the tin. Cover, then refrigerate until required.
3 Meanwhile, put all the filling ingredients in a bowl and whisk until smooth.
4 Pour the mixture into the tin and bake in the oven for 1 hour, until the cheesecake is only just firm.
5 Remove the cheesecake from the oven and leave to cool for 15 minutes.
6 Meanwhile, make the topping: mix the soured cream, sugar and vanilla until blended.
7 Pour the soured cream topping mixture over the cheesecake and return to the oven for 10 minutes (see Cook's Notes).
8 Leave to cool, then cover with foil and chill for at least 12, preferably 24, hours before serving.
9 To serve: run a knife around the sides of the cheesecake, then carefully remove the sides of the tin. Cut into slices.

COOK'S NOTES

Allow 30 minutes preparation, 1½ hours cooking, then cooling and chilling for at least 12 hours.

When the cheesecake is removed from the oven after stage 5, the soured cream topping will still be soft. It will firm up during the chilling time. Transport in the tin.

To crush the biscuits, put them in a strong polythene bag, a few at a time, and crush with a rolling pin on a work surface.

Mix whole and chopped hazelnuts in a small container to decorate just before serving.

● 585 calories/2450 kj per portion

Mango ice cream

SERVES 12
**750 g/1½ lb mangoes, prepared
weight (see Cook's Notes)**
**3 tablespoons fresh or bottled lemon
juice**
425 ml/¾ pint double cream
3 tablespoons sugar

1 Purée the mangoes in a blender or work them through a nylon sieve. Stir in the lemon juice.
2 Whip the cream with the sugar until it begins to form soft peaks, then fold into the mango purée.
3 Spoon the mixture into a rigid container and place in the freezer (see Cook's Notes). Freeze for about 3–4 hours, until firm.

4 Remove the ice cream from the freezer 15 minutes before serving, and allow to soften slightly at normal room temperature.
5 Scoop the ice cream into individual glasses to serve.

COOK'S NOTES

This dish takes 10 minutes to prepare and 3–4 hours to freeze.

Hold the mango over a plate to catch the juice and score the skin lengthways with a sharp knife, dividing it into several sections. Pull the skin away from each section, then close the flesh from the large central stone in large pieces. Scrape any remaining flesh from the skin and add to the slices with the juices.

If you do not have a freezer, you can make the ice cream in the freezing compartment of the refrigerator.

Turn it to its coldest setting at least 1 hour before making the ice cream, and remember to return it to its original setting when finished.

Take care not to whisk the cream too stiffly or the finished ice cream will have a waxy texture.

About 1 kg/2 lb fresh mangoes will provide 750 g/1½ lb flesh. If fresh ones are unavailable, three 425 g/15 oz cans well-drained mango slices will give you the correct amount of fruit.

● **195 calories/800 kj per portion**

Harvest pudding

SERVES 4–6

225 g/8 oz cooking plums, halved and stoned
500 lb/1 lb cooking apples, peeled, cored and sliced
275 g/10 oz sugar
225 g/8 oz fresh or frozen blackberries
8 trifle sponge cakes, cut in half horizontally
softly whipped cream, to serve (optional)

1 Put the plums, apples and 200 g/ 7 oz sugar into a heavy-based saucepan. Cover and cook gently for 10 minutes, stirring occasionally. Add the blackberries and remaining sugar, replace the lid and cook for a further 10 minutes, until all the fruit is very soft.

2 Turn the fruit into a nylon sieve set over a bowl to drain off juice.

3 Arrange a few slices of sponge cake in the base of a 1.5 L/2½ pint pudding basin. Cover the cake with a layer of fruit and sprinkle over about 1 tablespoon of the drained juice. Continue making layers in this way until all the cake and fruit are used, finishing with a layer of cake.

4 Stand the basin on a plate, then cover the pudding with cling film. Put a small plate or lid which fits just inside the rim of the basin on top of the pudding. Weight the plate down, then leave the pudding in the refrigerator overnight.

5 To serve: run a palette knife around the sides of the pudding to loosen it, then invert a serving plate on top. Hold the plate and basin firmly and invert, giving a sharp shake halfway round. Carefully lift off the basin and serve with cream.

COOK'S NOTES

Allow 40 minutes preparation, plus at least 8 hours chilling.

Take care not to add too much juice: if the pudding is very soggy it will collapse when turned out on the serving plate.

Do not throw the remaining juice away. It can be poured over the pudding after it has been turned out, or it can be kept in the refrigerator for 3–4 days and diluted with lemonade, cream soda or tonic water to make a delicious cold drink.

● 510 calories/2140 kj per portion

Pineapple biscuit pie

MAKES 6 SLICES

175 g/6 oz digestive biscuits
   (see Cook's Notes), finely crushed
2 tablespoons caster sugar
75 g/3 oz butter, melted

FILLING

150 g/5 oz tablet lemon jelly, cut
   into cubes
150 ml/¼ pint boiling water
225 g/8 oz can pineapple slices in
   natural juice, drained and
   chopped, with juice reserved
1 tablespoon lemon juice
175 g/6 oz can evaporated milk,
   chilled (see Cook's Notes)
'leaves' of angelica, to decorate
   (optional)

1 Put the biscuit crumbs into a bowl. Add the sugar and butter and mix well. Spoon into a loose-based 20 cm/8 inch flan tin and press evenly over the base and up the sides. Cover and refrigerate while you prepare the filling.

2 Put the jelly and water into a small saucepan and stir over very low heat until the jelly has dissolved. Remove from the heat.

3 Strain the pineapple juice into the jelly, then add the lemon juice and stir well to mix. Pour into a bowl and leave for about 3 hours or until on the point of setting (see Cook's Notes).

4 Whip the evaporated milk until thick and foamy, then whisk it into the jelly. Reserve some of the largest pineapple pieces. Using a large metal spoon, fold the remaining pineapple into the jelly, then chill for 15 minutes.

5 Remove the biscuit case from the tin and place on a serving plate. Pile the filling into the case, then decorate with the reserved pineapple and angelica, if liked. Serve as soon as possible.

COOK'S NOTES

Allow 15 minutes plus chilling time for the biscuit case, then 15 minutes plus setting for the filling.

Stale biscuits can be used, but for a crisp result, bake the prepared case in a 180C/350F/Gas 4 oven for 8–10 minutes, cool, then chill.

Evaporated milk will whip to a thick consistency if it has been chilled in the refrigerator for several hours beforehand. Keep a can in the refrigerator ready for this kind of dessert. To speed setting, cool the jelly, cover and refrigerate.

● 380 calories/1575 kj per slice

Blackcurrant marble

SERVES 6

1 rounded tablespoon (1 sachet)
  powdered gelatine
425 ml/¾ pint water
300 ml/½ pint concentrated
  blackcurrant health drink
  (see Cook's Notes)
150 ml/¼ pint double cream
150 g/5 oz natural yoghurt

1 Sprinkle the gelatine over 150 ml/
¼ pint of the water in a small heatproof bowl and leave to soak for
5 minutes until spongy.
2 Meanwhile, mix the blackcurrant
drink together with the remaining
water in a bowl.
3 Stand the bowl containing the
gelatine in a pan of gently simmering
water for 2–3 minutes, stirring
occasionally until the gelatine has
dissolved completely.
4 Stir the dissolved gelatine into
blackcurrant liquid (see Cook's
Notes). Cover and refrigerate the
liquid for about 2 hours, until the jelly

is just on the point of setting.
5 Whip the cream until it forms soft
peaks. Put half the blackcurrant jelly
into a large bowl, then fold in the
cream with a large metal spoon.
Whisk the yoghurt into the remaining
jelly.
6 Cover each mixture and return to
the refrigerator for 5–10 minutes,
until on the point of setting.
7 Lightly fold the blackcurrant yoghurt mixture through the creamy
blackcurrant mixture to give a
marbled effect. Cover and refrigerate
for a maximum of 8 hours until set.
8 To serve: scoop the dessert into
individual glass bowls. Serve chilled.

COOK'S NOTES

Allow 25 minutes preparation, plus
setting time.

Pour the gelatine in a thin stream
on to the blackcurrant liquid, stirring constantly. This prevents the
gelatine setting in threads on con-
tact with the cold liquid.

Do not overwork the two mix-
tures, or you will lose the pretty
marble effect.

Concentrated blackcurrant health
drink is sold in supermarkets.

● 240 calories/1000 kj per portion

104

Cranberry sherbet in apple cases

SERVES 6

2 × 180 g/6½ oz jars cranberry sauce
finely grated zest of 1 small orange
2 egg whites
6 green dessert apples
2 tablespoons lemon juice
apple leaves, to decorate (optional)

1 Press the cranberry sauce through a sieve into a bowl. Add the orange zest, stir well to mix, then refrigerate for 30 minutes.
2 In a clean dry bowl, whisk the egg whites until standing in soft peaks, then fold into the cranberry and orange mixture.
3 Pour into a shallow freezerproof container and freeze (see Cook's Notes) for about 1 hour or until the mixture is firm around the edges.
4 Remove from the freezer, turn out into a bowl and beat well until smooth. Return the mixture to the freezerproof container and continue to freeze for at least 4 hours until it is quite solid.
5 Remove sherbet from the freezer and stand at room temperature for about 30 minutes until it is soft enough to scoop.
6 Meanwhile, hollow out the centre of each apple to within 1 cm/½ inch of the base (see Cook's Notes). Immediately brush the insides of the apples with lemon juice and refrigerate until required.
7 Fill the apple cavities with scoops of the sherbet, stand on a baking sheet and return to the freezer for about 30 minutes until the apples begin to look frosty. Decorate with apple tops or leaves, if liked, and stand on individual plates. Serve.

COOK'S NOTES

You will need about 35 minutes to prepare sherbert and 5 hours freezing; then about 30 minutes to prepare apples and 30 minutes final freezing.

If using the freezing compartment of the refrigerator, turn to coldest setting 1 hour before you start making the sherbet. Do not forget to return it to the original setting.

To hollow out an apple proceed as follows: Cut top off apple then, using a sharp-edged teaspoon cut out core, leaving a 1 cm/½ inch thick shell.
● 170 calories/700 kj per portion

Tropical whip

COOK'S NOTES

SERVES 4

150 g/5 oz table lime jelly, cut into cubes

2 × 150 g/5 oz cartons tropical fruit yoghurt

grape 'waterlilies' to decorate

1 Place the jelly in a small saucepan and add 150 ml/¼ pint boiling water. Stir over very low heat until the jelly has completely dissolved, then remove from the heat and stir in 150 ml/¼ pint cold water.

2 Pour the jelly into a bowl and leave to cool for 10 minutes, then gradually whisk in the yoghurt, making sure it is evenly blended. Pour the whip into 4 serving glasses or small bowls. (There may be some bubbles on top.) Cover and refrigerate for at least 1 hour, until set.

3 Just before serving, decorate each whip with grape 'waterlilies'.

Allow 20 minutes preparation (including making the waterlilies), plus setting.

For packed lunches, set the whips in small polythene containers.

Use large grapes for the waterlilies and make them according to the method below:

1 Hold each grape on a board, stalk end down. Using a small sharp knife, make 3 diagonal cuts in each grape to give 6 sections, taking care not to cut right through the grapes.

2 Ease the cut sections open and carefully remove the pips, then place a small piece of green glacé cherry in the centre of the opened grape 'petals'.

This unusual yoghurt is flavoured with such delicious tropical fruits as pineapple, passion fruit, mango and guava; if difficult to obtain, use the supermarket brands of passion fruit and melon yoghurt.

● 165 calories/675 kj per portion

106

Rhubarb fool

SERVES 4

750 g/1½ lb rhubarb (see Cook's Notes), cut into 2.5 cm/1 inch lengths
100 g/4 oz caster sugar
finely grated zest and juice of ½ orange
150 ml/¼ pint whipping or double cream
few drops of red food colouring (optional)
brandy snaps or other crisp biscuits, to serve

1 Put the rhubarb, sugar, orange zest and juice into a heavy-based, aluminium or enamel-lined pan and mix well. Bring slowly to simmering point, then turn down the heat to low, cover and cook until the rhubarb is very tender (see Cook's Notes). Remove pan from the heat.
2 Turn the rhubarb mixture into a nylon sieve set over a bowl and leave until excess liquid has drained away. Purée the rhubarb in a blender, then pour into a clean bowl and leave to cool completely (see Cook's Notes).
3 Whisk the cream until standing in soft peaks. Using a large metal spoon, fold the cream into the rhubarb until evenly blended. Stir in a few drops of colouring, if liked.
4 Spoon into a serving bowl or 4 individual dishes. Cover and refrigerate for at least 1 hour. Serve chilled, with brandy snaps or other thin, crisp biscuits.

COOK'S NOTES

Preparation takes 25–35 minutes (depending on cooking time). Allow extra time for cooling and chilling.

Well-drained, defrosted rhubarb can be used; reduce the sugar if the rhubarb is already sweetened.

Cooking time depends on the age of the rhubarb. Allow about 10 minutes for tender, forced rhubarb and up to 30 minutes for mature stalks.

Taste the cold purée and add more sugar, if liked, but keep the rhubarb slightly tart and remember the cream will soften its acidity.

Add 2–3 teaspoons orange-flavoured liqueur to the cold purée; decorate with drained canned mandarin orange segments or twists of orange just before serving.

For a lighter dessert, use two 150 g/5 oz cartons of natural yoghurt instead of the cream.

Prepare up to the end of stage 3, then turn into a polythene container, cover tightly and refrigerate for up to 2 days. To serve: spoon into a bowl or 4 individual dishes.

● 235 calories/1000 kj per portion

Pineapple mallow

MAKES 8 SLICES
225 g/8 oz digestive biscuits, finely crushed
100 g/4 oz butter, melted
extra butter, for greasing

FILLING AND DECORATION
225 g/8 oz marshmallows, cut into pieces (see Cook's Notes)
125 ml/4 fl oz medium-dry white wine
376 g/13¼ oz can crushed pineapple, thoroughly drained, with syrup reserved
1 rounded tablespoon (1 sachet) powdered gelatine
4 tablespoons water
300 ml/½ pint double cream
drained pineapple rings and frosted mint (see Cook's Notes), to decorate

1 Butter a deep, 23 cm/9 inch round cake tin with a loose base. Mix together the biscuit crumbs and melted butter, then press evenly over base of prepared tin. Refrigerate while preparing the filling.

2 Place marshmallows, wine and pineapple syrup in a heavy saucepan. Stir over low heat until marshmallows have melted, then set aside.

3 Sprinkle the gelatine over the water in a small heatproof bowl. Leave to soak for 5 minutes until spongy, then stand the bowl in a pan of gently simmering water for 1–2 minutes, stirring occasionally, until the gelatine has dissolved.

4 Stir the gelatine into the marshmallow mixture, then turn the mixture into a large bowl and leave for about 20 minutes, until thickened but not set.

5 Whip the cream until standing in soft peaks, then fold it into the marshmallow mixture. Cover and refrigerate for about 30 minutes, until on the point of setting.

6 Pour half the mixture into the prepared tin, then carefully spoon the crushed pineapple over the top. Spread remaining mixture over the pineapple. Cover and refrigerate for at least 8 hours, until set.

7 To serve: remove sides of tin and place cake on a serving plate. Decorate with pineapple and mint.

COOK'S NOTES

Allow 45 minutes preparation, plus cooling, chilling and setting time.

To prevent sticking, dip the knife blade in hot water, or use lightly oiled kitchen scissors to snip the marshmallows into very small pieces.

Brush sprigs of mint with lightly beaten egg white, then dip in caster sugar. Dry on a wire rack.

● 540 calories/2250 kj per slice

Creamy lemon mousse

SERVES 4

2 eggs, separated
2 egg yolks
100 g/4 oz caster sugar
finely grated zest of 2 lemons and
 5 tablespoons lemon juice
50 g/2 oz butter, melted
150 ml/¼ pint double cream
thin slices of lemon, to decorate

1 Put the 4 egg yolks and caster sugar into a large bowl. Using a hand-held electric whisk (see Cook's Notes), beat together until pale, foamy and thick enough to hold the trail of the whisk for 3 seconds when the beaters are lifted from bowl.
2 Using a large metal spoon, gently fold in the lemon zest and juice and the melted butter.
3 In a clean, dry bowl and using clean beaters, whisk the egg whites until standing in stiff peaks. In a separate bowl, whip the cream until it forms soft peaks. Lightly fold the cream and then the egg whites into the egg yolk and lemon mixture.
4 Divide the mousse between 4 dessert glasses or bowls, cover with cling film and refrigerate for at least 30 minutes or up to 2 hours.
5 To serve: uncover and decorate with lemon slices. Serve chilled.

COOK'S NOTES

Allow 20 minutes preparation, plus up to 2 hours chilling time.
 If using a rotary whisk, put the egg yolk mixture in a heatproof bowl and whisk over barely simmering water. When the mixture will hold the trail of the whisk, remove the bowl from the pan and whisk until completely cool.

● 460 calories/1925 kj per portion

Tropical creams

SERVES 4

225 g/8 oz can pineapple slices in natural juice, drained and chopped with juice reserved

about 175 ml/6 fl oz orange and passion fruit juice (see Cook's Notes)

1 rounded tablespoon (1 sachet) powdered gelatine

3 eggs

50 g/2 oz caster sugar

15 g/½ oz drained stem ginger, finely chopped

75 ml/3 fl oz double cream

1 Make up the pineapple juice to 300 ml/½ pint with orange and passion fruit juice. Put 3 tablespoons of the mixed juice into a heatproof bowl, sprinkle over the gelatine and leave to soak.

2 Meanwhile, separate 2 of the eggs.

3 Put the egg yolks, remaining egg and sugar into a large bowl. Using a table-top mixer (see Cook's Notes),

beat until the mixture is thick enough to retain the impression of the whisk for 3 seconds when the beaters are lifted.

4 Stand the bowl containing the gelatine in a pan of gently simmering water and leave, stirring occasionally, for 1–2 minutes, until the gelatine is dissolved.

5 Whisk the gelatine into the egg mixture, then whisk in the mixed fruit juice. Leave in a cool place for about 15 minutes, until beginning to set (see Cook's Notes).

6 Using clean beaters, whisk the egg whites until standing in stiff peaks. Fold the egg whites into the gelatine mixture. Reserve some pineapple for decoration; fold the rest into the mixture with the ginger.

7 Divide between 4 glass bowls, making sure the fruit is evenly distributed. Cover and refrigerate for 1 hour, or until set.

8 To serve: whip the cream until it forms soft peaks, then pipe or spoon over each serving. Decorate with the reserved pineapple.

COOK'S NOTES

Preparation (including initial setting time) takes 35–45 minutes. Final setting time is about 1 hour.

Pure orange and passion fruit juice is sold in 500 ml/18 fl oz cartons in large supermarkets. If unavailable, use unsweetened orange juice.

If you do not have a table-top mixer, use a rotary or hand-held electric whisk and beat over hot water. If mixture separates, whisk before adding egg whites.

● 265 calories/1100 kj per portion

Blackcurrant sorbet

SERVES 4

**250 g/9 oz fresh or frozen
blackcurrants without stalks**
100 g/4 oz sugar
**300 ml/¼ pint water, plus
2 tablespoons**
2 teaspoons lemon juice
½ teaspoon powdered gelatine
1 egg white

1 Put the sugar and 300 ml/½ pint water in a heavy-based pan and heat gently until the sugar has dissolved. Boil for 10 minutes until syrupy, then remove from the heat and set aside to cool.

2 Put the blackcurrants in a pan with the lemon juice and heat gently for about 10 minutes until softened. Allow to cool slightly, then purée in a blender. Press the puréed blackcurrants through a sieve into a bowl to remove seeds and skin.

3 Sprinkle the gelatine over the 2 tablespoons water in a heatproof bowl and leave to soak for 5 minutes until spongy. Stand the bowl in a pan of gently simmering water and heat gently for 1–2 minutes stirring occasionally until the gelatine has dissolved. Stir the gelatine into the cooled sugar syrup, making sure it has completely dissolved.

4 Stir the sugar syrup into the blackcurrant purée and mix well. Turn into a rigid container and freeze, uncovered (see Cook's Notes), for about 3 hours until the mixture is firm around the edges but not frozen in the middle of the dish.

5 Remove the blackcurrant mixture from the freezer and break up with a fork. Whisk the egg white until it stands in stiff peaks, then fold into the blackcurrant mixture. Cover and freeze overnight, until solid.

6 To serve, stand at room temperature for about 30 minutes until the sorbet is soft enough to scoop into the reserved individual glasses.

COOK'S NOTES

Allow 45 minutes preparation plus 3 hours initial freezing time, then freezing overnight.

If using the freezing compartment of the refrigerator, turn it to its coldest setting 1 hour before making the sorbet. Return it to the original setting afterwards.

Serve the sorbet with small meringues or with crisp French biscuits.

Seal, label and freeze for up to 3 months.

● **125 calories/525 kj per portion**

Apple flummery

SERVES 4
2 large eggs, separated
50 g/2 oz sugar
600 ml/1 pint milk
25 g/1 oz semolina
pinch of salt
1 large cooking apple, weighing about 300 g/11 oz, peeled, cored and puréed
juice of ½ small lemon

TO SERVE
1 red-skinned dessert apple
few drops of lemon juice

1 Put the egg yolks and sugar in a bowl and beat together until creamy.
2 Put the milk into a large saucepan and warm it over moderate heat. Sprinkle in the semolina and bring to the boil, stirring constantly to avoid sticking.
3 Add the salt and lower the heat, then simmer for 10 minutes, stirring constantly.
4 Gradually stir in the egg yolk and sugar mixture until well mixed, then continue cooking very gently for a further 2 minutes, stirring all the time. Do not allow the mixture to boil or it will stick to the bottom of the pan and may burn.
5 Remove the pan from the heat, then stir in the apple purée and lemon juice until well blended with the rest of the mixture.
6 Whisk the egg whites until stiff and fold into the mixture in the pan, using a metal spoon.
7 Carefully spoon the mixture into individual glasses and leave to cool for about 30 minutes.
8 To serve: thinly slice the apple, discarding the core, but leaving the skin on. Sprinkle immediately with lemon juice to prevent discoloration. Place a few slices on each serving and then serve the flummery at once.

COOK'S NOTES

Cooking time is about 50 minutes, including 15 minutes to prepare and purée the apple.

The flummery is a particularly light and refreshing desert — it separates slightly into a shallow layer of liquid at the bottom, topped with a fluffy mixture.

According to the dictionary, flummery is an old Welsh word of unknown derivation, but it refers to a traditional sweet dish (popular in the British Isles) which is milk and egg-based and which is always traditionally eaten cold.

● **250 calories/1050 kj per portion**

Strawberry yoghurt freeze

SERVES 6
500 g/1 lb strawberries, hulled
450 g/16 oz natural yoghurt
1½ teaspoons powdered gelatine
125 ml/4 fl oz water
175 g/6 oz caster sugar

1 Reserve 6 small strawberries for decoration. Work the remaining strawberries through a nylon sieve, or purée in a blender, then sieve to remove the seeds. Using a fork, stir the yoghurt into the purée until it is evenly combined.

2 Sprinkle the gelatine over the water in a small, heavy-based pan. Leave to soak for 5 minutes until spongy, then set over very low heat for 1–2 minutes until the gelatine is completely dissolved.

3 Add the sugar and stir until it is dissolved, remove from the heat and leave to cool for 5 minutes.

4 Stir a little of the strawberry yog-hurt into the gelatine mixture, then pour on to the bulk of the strawberry yoghurt, stirring all the time (see Cook's Notes).

5 Pour the mixture into a 1.5 L/2½ pint rigid plastic container, cover and freeze for about 3 hours or until frozen around the edges.

6 Turn the mixture into a bowl and whisk until smooth. Return to the container, cover and freeze for a further 8 hours, or overnight, until firm.

7 To serve: transfer the container to the main part of the refrigerator for approximately 1 hour, or until the yoghurt ices have softened. Spoon into small dishes and decorate with the reserved strawberries. Serve the yoghurt ices at once, before they start to melt.

COOK'S NOTES

Preparation takes about 40 minutes plus freezing time.

Blending the gelatine with a little of the cold strawberry yoghurt prevents it 'roping' (setting in strings).

Keep the heat very low and remove the pan immediately the sugar is dissolved. If gelatine boils it will be unusable.

Store in the freezer for 3 months.
● 185 calories/775 kj per portion

SUMMER DRINKS

Peachy pinkers

MAKES 16 DRINKS
1 block of ice
200 ml/7 fl oz grenadine
75 cl/1½ pint bottle rosé wine,
 chilled
600 ml/1 pint sparkling water,
 chilled
crushed ice or ice cubes, to serve

FOR THE DECORATION
225 g/8 oz fresh peaches
2 tablespoons lemon juice
mint or borage sprigs

1 Place the block of ice in a large serving bowl and pour over the grenadine. Pour in the rosé wine and stir to mix well.
2 Stone the peaches, slice them thinly and toss the slices in lemon juice, then add to the bowl.
3 Just before serving pour on the mineral water, stir again and add the sprigs of mint or borage.

4 Put crushed ice or ice cubes into each glass and ladle in the drink, making sure that each serving has a slice of fruit and a sprig of herbs.

COOK'S NOTES

This drink only takes 15 minutes to prepare but needs to be thoroughly chilled.

For a non-alcoholic but equally delicious drink, use fizzy lemonade in place of the wine and add more grenadine to taste.

For a pinky-purple variation of this drink use cassis in place of the grenadine and a medium-sweet white wine in place of the rosé. Decorate the rim of the bowl with small bunches of grapes and add a few grapes to each glass when serving.

Party punch

MAKES 8 PINTS
700 ml/1¼ pints clear lemon juice
350 g/12 oz brown sugar
2 bottles Jamaican rum
1 bottle brandy
1.75 L/3 pints cold water
175 ml/6 fl oz peach bitters
275 g/10 oz fresh and peeled or canned and drained sliced peaches, roughly chopped

1 Place the lemon juice and sugar in a large punch bowl. Stir well to dissolve the sugar. Add the rum, brandy, water, bitters and peaches. Stir well to combine the ingredients.

2 Leave the punch to stand for at least 3 hours, stirring occasionally.
3 Put a large block of ice in the bowl to really chill the drink and serve in glasses or punch cups.

COOK'S NOTES

This punch needs to be made at least 3 hours before you start drinking to let all the ingredients mix properly together.

This is quite a strong punch but is an ideal drink for summer parties.

Serve the punch bowl outside in the garden and let guests help themselves using a ladle.

Buck's fizz

SERVES 12

4 × 75 cl/1½ pint bottles dry Champagne (see Cook's Notes)
3.5 L/5 pints orange juice

1 Chill the Champagne and orange juice, plus 12 Champagne glasses (see Cook's Notes) and a large water jug.
2 To serve: pour the orange juice into the chilled jug. Half fill each glass with orange juice, then top up with Champagne.

COOK'S NOTES

Allow a total of about 2 hours chilling time.

For a true Buck's fizz, real Champagne must be used, but a good sparkling white wine, or even a dry cider, make less expensive substitutes.

Champagne should be served in tall narrow glasses, which help retain the bubbles and prevent it from quickly going flat. Another way to use Champagne in a mixed drink is with brandy, as a Champagne cocktail.

Mix the cocktail just before serving so it will be bubbly.

Serve a fizzy mixture of orange juice and soda, or lemonade or tonic water for children.

116

Summer cup

SERVES 6–8

2 tablespoons clear honey
75 cl/1½ pint bottle dry white wine
125 ml/4 fl oz brandy
125 ml/4 fl oz mead or cider
700 ml/1¼ pints lemonade
1 orange, sliced
1 lemon, sliced
1 ripe pear, peeled, cored and sliced

1 In a small saucepan, heat the honey and one-quarter of the wine over moderate heat, stirring until the honey has dissolved.

2 Remove the pan from the heat and pour the honey mixture into a punch bowl or large jug. Stir in the remaining wine, the brandy, mead or cider and lemonade. Add the orange, lemon and pear slices.

3 Chill the cup in the refrigerator for 2 hours. If the bowl or jug is too large to fit in the refrigerator, add 12 ice cubes to the mixture, cover and leave to stand in a cool place.

4 To serve, place 2 or 3 ice cubes in each glass and pour the mixture over them. Serve immediately.

COOK'S NOTES

A total of about 2 hours chilling time is needed.

This is a sweet, but very pleasant and refreshing summer drink and is ideal for serving with a barbecue buffet on a hot evening.

Make sure you add the extra ice cubes before serving the cup to appreciate its true flavour.

Kid's kooler

SERVES 4

12 ice cubes
**350 ml/12 fl oz unsweetened
    pineapple juice, chilled**
**few drops of fresh lime juice
    (see Cook's Notes)**
**350 ml/12 fl oz unsweetened orange
    juice, chilled**
**2 tablespoons grenadine syrup
    (see Cook's Notes)**

TO GARNISH (OPTIONAL)

**½ slice fresh pineapple with skin, or
    4 canned pineapple pieces,
    drained**
2 slices lime
2 small slices orange
8 maraschino or glacé cherries

1 Prepare the garnish, if using: cut the pineapple slice into quarters to make 4 triangular wedges. Cut each slice of citrus fruit into halves. On each of 4 cocktail sticks, spear 1 cherry followed by 1 piece each of lime, pineapple and orange, then another cherry.

2 Make the drinks: put 3 ice cubes into the bottom of 4 highball glasses or tall 225 ml/8 fl oz tumblers. Pour 75 ml/3 fl oz pineapple juice into each glass, add a squeeze of lime, then 75 ml/3 fl oz orange juice.

3 Pour a thin stream of grenadine, straight from the bottle, in a circle around the edge of each drink. (The grenadine will sink to form a rosy layer at the bottom of the glass.)

4 Garnish the drinks with the prepared fruits, by balancing a cocktail stick across the top of each glass. Put 1–2 long straws into each drink and serve at once.

COOK'S NOTES

Total preparation time (including the garnish) is about 10 minutes.

For an adult Kooler with a kick, replace some or all of the pineapple juice with gin or vodka.

Grenadine is a bright red sweet syrup, flavoured with pomegranate juice. It is used to colour, flavour and sweeten some potent cocktails, notably Tequila Sunrise. The bottle has a special top so you can pour the syrup straight into the drinks.

Some brands of grenadine contain a little alcohol; buy the non-alcoholic kind.

A small dash of lime juice heightens and intensifies the flavour of pineapple.

Zombie cocktail

SERVES 1
50 ml/2 fl oz light rum
50 ml/2 fl oz dark rum
3 tablespoons lime juice
2 tablespoons pineapple juice
1 teaspoon sugar
2 ice cubes
1 Maraschino cherry

1 Chill a medium-sized cocktail glass in the refrigerator for 30 minutes.
2 Meanwhile, place all of the ingredients, except the ice cubes, in a cocktail shaker or screw-top jar. Cover and shake the mixture vigorously for about 1 minute.
3 Remove the glass from the refrigerator and add the ice cubes. Pour over the cocktail mixture and decorate with the cherries. Serve the cocktail at once.

COOK'S NOTES

This is a very quick drink to make, but chilling a cocktail glass in the refrigerator first makes all the difference.

As this drink contains quite a potent mixture of ingredients you can lessen its effect by adding some water to it and some more ice cubes.

If you have several people coming make up the required ingredients to suit the numbers.

119

INDEX